REYNOLDS PRICE

A WHOLE NEW LIFE

An Illness and a Healing

A PLUME BOOK

PLUME
Published by the Penguin Group
Penguin Books USA Inc., 375 Hudson Street, New York, New York 10014, U.S.A.
Penguin Books Ltd, 27 Wrights Lane, London W8 5TZ, England
Penguin Books Australia Ltd, Ringwood, Victoria, Australia
Penguin Books Canada Ltd, 10 Alcorn Avenue, Toronto, Ontario, Canada M4V 3B2
Penguin Books (N.Z.) Ltd, 182–190 Wairau Road, Auckland 10, New Zealand

Penguin Books Ltd, Registered Offices: Harmondsworth, Middlesex, England

Published by Plume, an imprint of Dutton Signet,
a division of Penguin Books USA Inc.
This is an authorized reprint of a hardcover edition published by Atheneum.
For information address Simon & Schuster,
866 Third Avenue, New York, NY 10022.

First Plume Printing, June, 1995
10 9 8

Ⓟ REGISTERED TRADEMARK—MARCA REGISTRADA

LIBRARY OF CONGRESS CATALOGING-IN-PUBLICATION DATA
Price, Reynolds
A whole new life / Reynolds Price.
p.   cm.
ISBN 0-452-27473-7
1. Price, Reynolds. —Health.   2. Novelists,
American—20th century—Biography.   3. Cancer—Patients—United
States—Biography.   4. Large type books.   I. Title.
[PS3566.R54Z477   1994c]
813'.54—dc20   94-48471
                                                          CIP

Printed in the United States of America

BOOKS ARE AVAILABLE AT QUANTITY DISCOUNTS WHEN USED TO PROMOTE PRODUCTS
OR SERVICES. FOR INFORMATION PLEASE WRITE TO PREMIUM MARKETING DIVISION,
PENGUIN BOOKS USA INC., 375 HUDSON STREET, NEW YORK, NEW YORK 10014.

BOOKS BY

REYNOLDS PRICE

A WHOLE NEW LIFE   1994

THE COLLECTED STORIES   1993

FULL MOON   1993

BLUE CALHOUN   1992

THE FORESEEABLE FUTURE   1991

NEW MUSIC   1990

THE USE OF FIRE   1990

THE TONGUES OF ANGELS   1990

CLEAR PICTURES   1989

GOOD HEARTS   1988

A COMMON ROOM   1987

THE LAWS OF ICE   1986

KATE VAIDEN   1986

PRIVATE CONTENTMENT   1984

MUSTIAN   1983

VITAL PROVISIONS   1982

THE SOURCE OF LIGHT   1981

A PALPABLE GOD   1978

EARLY DARK   1977

THE SURFACE OF EARTH   1975

THINGS THEMSELVES   1972

PERMANENT ERRORS   1970

LOVE AND WORK   1968

A GENEROUS MAN   1966

THE NAMES AND FACES OF HEROES   1963

A LONG AND HAPPY LIFE   1962

For
WILL PRICE, MY BROTHER
AND
ALLAN FRIEDMAN
AND
DANIEL VOLL

TO THE READER

THIS is a book about a mid-life collision with cancer and paralysis, a collision I've survived for ten years and counting. It means to be an accurate and readable account of a frightening painful time that ended; but while I know that any account of human realities will travel best in the form of a story, a compelling story is not my first aim. That aim is to give, in the midst of an honest narrative, a true record of the visible and invisible ways in which one fairly normal creature entered a trial, not of his choosing, and emerged after a long four years on a new life—a life that's almost wholly changed from the old. The record is offered first to others in physical or psychic trials of their own, to their families and other helpers and then to the curious reader who waits for his or her own devastation.

Not that I think I have special wisdom or that all my experience may prove useful for others in similar trouble; I assuredly don't. At best I'm a companionable voice that's lasted beyond all rational expectation. My ongoing life then may be a fact that others can lean on in their own ways, however briefly. In my worst times I'd have given a lot to hear from veterans of the kind of ordeal I was trapped in.

I've also worked to show not only the weight of the ordeal but the luck I found right through it—in friends and kin, in medical care (though with daunting exceptions), in my two kinds of work and in the now appalling, now astonishing grace of God. The human care at least was so steady that I understand how numerous others in worse straits may read this as the story of an insulated man in a skirmish.

But with all the gifts of luck and help that came down on me, the skirmish felt like total war. It does today, these years down the line. The bigger assaults of fear and pain, in whatever life they crash against, are indiscriminately strong. Only one creature bears the brunt; and the brunt slams down with no regard to the quality of the roof overhead, the cooking that's served or the presence of love or solitude. All the care and cash on Earth, however welcome, are a flimsy shield when the prospect of agonized death leans in.

My resources in writing this memoir were personal recall, questions to friends who witnessed the time, the regular calendar I kept and the poems, plays and fiction I wrote through the years in question. I also benefited from keen-eyed readings of the manuscript by my friends Erik Benson, Jared Burden, Alec Wilkinson and Daniel Voll. At no point did I ask to see my voluminous medical charts or ask any doctor to check my version. From the start of the trouble, I made a conscious choice not to open my file and confront what doctors believed was the worst—I saw in their eyes that they had slim hope, and I knew I must defy them. On balance I think the choice of a high degree of ignorance proved good for me. All my life I've tended to try to meet people's hopes. Predict my death and I'm liable to oblige; keep me ignorant and I stand a chance of lasting.

Short of searching my medical record then, what I still

know is how I felt and acted at the time and what I got in the way of help or bafflement from doctors and friends. I've likewise tried to make clear what a difficult patient and friend I was through much of the time. The dedication is offered to those three friends, from an unexpected plenty, who helped most and longest.

In any personal record that covers ten years, errors of fact and belief are inevitable. I've worked to hold them to a faithful minimum. Conversations are reported to the best of my recollection; I tape-recorded no one. The actual names of helpful people are given; others are identified by letters of the alphabet, roles or jobs, and I've been ruthless where I thought that was fair. When doctors and others who commit themselves to a life in medicine fail to respond to their patients as their own equals in need and feeling, then they're launched on a course whose destination is bleak to consider—the human being as laboratory animal. While the sight of illness elicits the best from many people, the always astounding fact remains that the sight of sustained illness heightens the blundering cruelty of some. But since the giving of thanks in many quarters is another big aim here, I ask for pardon from any quarters where I've been unjust.

Pardon too if at times I seem to award myself small medals for deportment. Any survivor of a long ordeal will know that no one makes it on pure good luck or the backs of others; and in the glare of that knowledge, either some degree of self-confidence grows or the mind disintegrates rapidly. Concealing that awareness would only be a form of deceit. I well understand that all ground won is won for the moment, and I trust it's clear that my confidence is shaky.

R.P., 1994

1

So far it had been the best year of my life. In love and friendship I was lavishly endowed. I'd recently published a new play—my twelfth book in the twenty-two years since my first, A *Long and Happy Life*. They'd all been received more generously than not by the nation's book journalists and buyers. I'd been steadily rewarded with understanding readers of many kinds; and I'd earned a sizable income from a brand of work that was mostly deep pleasure in the doing. For twenty-six years I'd also taught English literature and narrative writing at Duke University. The annual one semester's work with good students was not a financial necessity for me but a test of sanity against the touchstone of merciless young minds. I'd lived for nearly two decades, alone by choice, in an ample house by a pond and woods that teemed with wildlife; and in February I'd turned fifty-one, apparently hale.

The previous fall, October '83, I'd gone with a friend to Israel. It was my second visit in three years to a place that had fed my curiosity since childhood and was promising now to enter my work. To save at least some of the goodness of the year, I'd begun to keep a daybook called *Days and Nights*. It consisted of quickly written poems, each triggered by some aspect of the pile-up of happiness and recompense in the long calm days.* By the spring of 1984 I'd finished the first third of my sixth novel, *Kate Vaiden*.

But as the son of a father who'd always doubted his rare good luck and who died at fifty-four, I'd begun to hear occasional ominous chords. In all the elation of recent months, I somehow knew I was on a thin-aired precipice. I knew I'd come down gently or hard; and by early April the daybook poems, more alert than I, were well aware that an end was near. One poem called "Caw" even sounds a knell for the run of luck.

> *Splayed face-down on the last pool of sleep,*
> *I'm gaffed by caw-caw from one distant crow.*
> *What Roman would rise to face this day?*
>
> *Half an hour later I loom at the pond window,*
> *Glum while my two globes of barnyard cholesterol*
> *Gurgle behind me in salt-free fat*
>
> *To the tune of the radio voice of Charles Simic*
> *Who suddenly flings out a cold crow poem.*
> *What human would join me to face this day?*

But I barely listened to the curious warnings, and the next few poems are about new love. My main response to the racing days still had to be thanks, thanks and the care to save these memories against an ending.

Then on a clear day in mid-April, I was walking through the crowded Duke campus with a friend and

---

* All the daybook poems appear in my volumes *The Laws of Ice* (Atheneum, 1986) and *The Use of Fire* (Atheneum, 1990).

colleague, George Williams, a man more watchful than most. After a few silent yards, he said "Why are you slapping your left foot on the pavement?"

I laughed at what seemed a rare error in his observations and said that I wasn't—I was wearing thong sandals that tended to shuffle. But I took a few more steps and heard he was right. This was no shuffle; I was lifting my left foot higher than usual and slapping it stiffly down on the pavement. If I thought the motion was more than odd at the time, I didn't act on it or begin to worry.

A few days later in my neighborhood video-rental store, I was laughing with the manager about our mutual plight as temperance fiends in a nation drunk on exercise. She said she'd started to jog at home on a stationary platform beside the TV. On the spot I tried to jog a few steps in place. My right leg wouldn't flex back off the floor. I could easily pull the foot backward with my hand and touch it to the back of my thigh, but on its own it couldn't respond to a mental command—*couldn't* or *wouldn't*? Before I could register puzzlement, my friend said "You're even worse off than me."

We laughed and dropped it, but later that day I phoned the cardiovascular-health unit at Duke to ask about joining a new middle-aged exercise group in which a few of my contemporaries were already thumping and jerking and lunching on sprouts.

And that same evening I started at least to face what I believed was the problem. I was just past fifty-one years old, weighing 167—thirty pounds more than I'd weighed in high school. In measuring my height recently, I'd discovered that I'd somehow lost an inch—I was now five-nine. Age was firmly staking its claims; I was starting to soften. For several years, when walking down stairs, I'd felt a sense of risky balance—I'd sometimes even take the arm of the person beside me—but I chalked that queasiness up to the bifocal glasses I'd worn in recent years.

Over the past months I'd also noticed a slowing down in sexual need and exertions; and though that need had won me a large part of the pleasures of my life, oddly the slowing didn't alarm me. I didn't feel unmanned, I didn't feel compelled to retire prematurely from an ongoing joy, I felt a natural change under way and was ready to let it define its course. Then in roaming the steep hills of Israel, I'd damaged the cartilage in one of my knees, but that eased quickly once I was home and took a few weeks of an anti-inflammatory drug.

From memories of my own father's early fifties, and from watching older male friends through the years, I'd assumed such losses came with the territory. Hadn't Father often fulminated that "These damned bifocals will kill me yet"; and hadn't my mother always said "After forty, it's maintenance, maintenance, maintenance"? Well, now I'd need to admit there were problems and begin to confront them. But the prospect of regular huffing and puffing with squads of garrulous heart-attack survivors in designer sweat suits was hardly beckoning, so I pushed the unattractive details of the cardiac-health unit to the back of my desk. Drastic remedies didn't seem called for. I'd handle this aging body on my own.

On my own had been the motto of most of my life—in exercise, in work and much else. As a boy who spent his early childhood with no brothers or sisters and no playmates, I'd missed an early exposure to communal games. My pastimes were mostly solitary. And once we moved into town among other boys when I was in the third grade, I was soon aware not only of my inexperience on teams but also of a full set of butterfingers at the ends of both arms. I caught and threw badly; and after a burst of

4

hard play, I'd often need to stand very still till my jumbled vision and whirling head could take their bearings. By the age of nine, with the private help of an older boy, I'd grown into a dependable touch-football lineman, a middling batter in softball; and later I became a roller-skate ace; but I loved none of them and was often the last team-member chosen from a motley pool. So once I was past compulsory gym class in high school and college, I gladly quit the playing fields.

Even in the bone-chilling torpor of my graduate years in the Thames valley of England, where I'd gone on a scholarship that expected physical vigor of me, exercise was never more strenuous than the odd walk or occasional swim. Generally I saw both activities as pointless interruptions of all that mattered, which were love and work—friends often called me "The Great Indoorsman." And now, by the early eighties, the exercise fads of the 1970s were alarmingly widespread. In the late seventies I'd bought my first pair of running shoes and glumly circled my big upper pasture for a few months at the urging of an orthopedist whom I consulted about a stiff lower back. But I soon gave in to the boredom and bugs and retired the shoes. Surely this new flock of driven joggers and jerkers were insuring a future of agonized joints. Why not take comfort in the memory of my numerous kin on both sides of my family? They'd been virtually motionless through long lives yet were clearheaded straight to their fully dressed deaths. So *sure, start working it out on your own, but gradually*.

By the end of April '84 though, I'd got two more warnings. On the night of the final examination in my Milton class, I made myself a sandwich at home and ate it quickly with one gin and tonic—two ounces of gin.

5

When I parked in the dusk and set off toward the building where my students waited for seven o'clock, I was startled to feel that I was nearly drunk. All my life I'd had a glass head for even small amounts of alcohol, but this slip on a class night was unprecedented. I took the firmest grip I could get on my faculties, proceeded across campus with the exaggerated caution of a Chaplinesque souse and gave the exam. No one seemed to notice; and before the students were done three hours later, my equilibrium had returned, though my sense had deepened that something was eerie.

Two days later as I parked on campus again to return final grades, I glanced at my watch and saw it was nearly five o'clock; the registrar's office would close on the dot. I should hurry along. I know I thought *Run*, a conscious signal, but I couldn't run. The command had got no farther than my brain. Some bridge was out. I stalled like a man on a menacing plain in a nightmare, inexplicably paralyzed. In a moment however I found I could walk at normal speed, though I had to concentrate not to veer or stumble.

I was concerned but still not quite scared enough to mention the newness to any friend or to see a doctor. I'd seen the needless punishment my parents took in their sad deaths, and I'd skirted doctors whenever I could. Again I reminded myself that I was just a man in broad mid-life with the muscle tone of a raw scallop. I still wouldn't join the old puffer-bellies at cardiac care. I'd start again jogging in the buggy pasture and cycling on the stationary bike I'd bought a few years back and quickly abandoned. And I really applied myself to the bike, half an hour twice a day. My legs obeyed me on the go-nowhere pedals, but after each session I'd feel like an octogenarian who's barely survived collision with a brick wall. I'd yet to feel any trace of pain, just immense exhaustion.

A quickly written poem in the daybook tries to paper

over the widening chasm. It describes my fatigue and ends with

> Rest. *The promise of a week like silt*
> *In a sweetwater delta, stirred only by minnows*
> *And the mutter of each slow skin of nacre*
> *As it welds to the pearl of a somnolent oyster—*
>
> *Mindless companion while I too mutter*
> *Round my gritty core, this ruined glad life.*

I'd give myself that week of rest, then return to work on my novel *Kate Vaiden*. With any luck I'd have it finished by the end of the year.

The relaxation and busywork on the indoor bike eased my mind, despite the fact that in public I had to pay even closer attention to walking straight and that I'd begun to dwell on two words in the night—*multiple sclerosis*, a generally slow process in which the body's immune cells attack the protective sheathing of the nerves and produce effects that range in severity from blurred vision and mild numbness to blindness and total paralysis. An old friend of mine had it in a bad form. She lived in a wheelchair now; and I'd visited her recently to find that her husband had moved out, leaving her alone and vulnerable in an insecure house. So her plight was a fearsome possibility; but on down toward the end of May, I went about my work and friendships with no concession to the gathering weakness and with surely no thought of seeing a doctor.

Then on Saturday, May 26th, I served as best man at the wedding of my friends Jeffrey Anderson and Lettie Randall—a fine mild afternoon, the guests uphill beneath a tent, live music beyond us in the trees. When the moment came to climb the incline toward the tent, Jeff motioned to me and led the way. I fell in beside him but by the third stride, I was in real trouble. There was no pain or dizziness, no fear of falling, just the fact that my legs were barely hearing my will to walk. I honestly didn't think I'd make it up the gentle slope. But some old overdrive kicked in, and somehow I was there at last on level ground with the bride and groom. The service went on and at the reception no one seemed to have noticed my trouble, so I laughed my way through a bibulous hour. *But how much of this is in my mind?*

On the Monday afternoon I went to a humane physician, an internist at Duke Hospital, a man slightly younger than I. He spent five minutes checking my reflexes with a rubber hammer. The responses looked normal to me. But the doctor stepped out and came back immediately with a staff neurologist, who repeated the check—no words between them. Then both men went out and shut the door; three minutes later they were back, poker-faced. Some of my long-nerve tracts were blocked. I'd need to come in for further tests, "a complete neurological work-up."

I said I was off to New York in a few days for a week's business but would then be free.

They glanced at each other; and the internist said "No, we need you now." I noted that they needed *me*, not that I needed *them*.

The neurologist stood in silence, nodding blankly.

That was my first real body blow from fear. *They're in earnest. This is big.* I recall that the cramped examining room seemed near to exploding with excess light.

*

I've had very little success through the years in my efforts at keeping a journal. In numerous attempts since adolescence, the process has left me even more detached and introspective than is natural for a bookish ex-boy who became a lone writer through most of his youth and adult life. For me, despite sporadic tries at a diary, my writing life has found sufficient pleasure in managing characters in fiction and plays. It's left slim need to manipulate friends to perform more interestingly for their next appearance in a journal. And the tedium of rehashing an uneventful day at the desk has likewise discouraged me—most productive writers live calmer lives than winkles.

But since the late 1950s when I got my first job teaching, I've needed simple daily calendars. And I've saved them all since, while they mostly record nothing more momentous than who I saw at dinner, I've sometimes noted a crucial event. Unlike the daybook of poems that I'd lately been keeping however, my calendar for May '84 shows oddly no suspicion of the growing strangeness in my body till it summarizes the doctors' advice on the 28th—"my immediate entry in hospital for neurological tests." It adds that I phoned two friends that evening with the news. Then alone I watched the film *All That Jazz*, a choice that proved inappropriate—there's a gruesomely depicted fatal surgery near the end.

But I have no memory of feelings from that night, the following day or the next half-day before I entered the hospital on Wednesday, May 30th '84. The calendar shows that on Tuesday morning, for encouragement, I phoned a friend who was studying in South Africa; and I met a friend at noon for lunch and another for dinner that night, after which—alone again—I watched another film, *The Last Wave*, a humorless Australian fantasy.

Surely during that hollow pause my mind must have run the odds time after time—multiple sclerosis, brain tumor, an inoperable cerebral aneurysm of the sort that had blinded and killed my mother. And since I've been an unorthodox non-churchly believer all my life, I must have prayed for stamina and mercy. I must have phoned my brother Bill in Raleigh, the man who'd bear the brunt of my care if care were needed. I know I told very few other people; that could wait for a clear diagnosis.

Yet from here I can read my sense of omen in the fact that I wrote no daybook poem on the prospect of my first hospital stay in twenty-nine years, and I made no other calendar notes beyond the bare facts of time and place. Of the Wednesday itself I only recall that my friend and fellow writer Elizabeth Cox came to my house in midafternoon. She'd offered to drive me in for the tests; I'd leave my car at home for safety. I took up my overnight bag, and Betsy and I paused in the yard to register the weird dull-pewter light from a partial eclipse of the spring sun which we watched in safety through a pinprick filter that I'd just made with two shirt-cardboards.

Then we rode four miles to Duke Hospital North, a big new complex on a street I'd traveled thousands of times since I'd come to town as a college freshman. As I left the car on my own steam, I moved again in the still-strange light of the eclipse. Recalling my boyhood reading about the superstitions of ancient Romans, I laughed back to Betsy and said something like "No self-respecting Roman would do this in a real eclipse." But I took my bag and walked through the wide doors, wobbly though upright, still with no trace of pain—my last free walk.

After the usual welcoming session with a sullen admissions clerk in the lobby, I was installed in a private room on the neurology ward. Once I'd provided a painless technician with unnervingly large amounts of fresh blood, I was interviewed by an especially confident young resident—the usual family history back to Adam and stage-comic questions to explore my sanity: "What day is this? Who's the president of the United States?"

Like most of the sane, I tried to answer amusingly; the resident was too young not to laugh. So only at the end of his clipboard of questions, when I crossed my right leg over my left and exposed my naked heel, did gravity reassert its grip.

The resident leaned down, touched a spot in the soft of my heel, stared for five seconds and said "That's called vermiculation."

As a Latin student I knew that words containing the syllable *verm-* tend to involve *worms*; and when I looked, the skin he'd touched was writhing steadily in silent tremors as if a knot of thin worms just under the surface was boiling upward. I asked what it meant.

He said "In general, pressure on nerves."

Someway I stayed even-keeled after that. The legacy of physical dread I'd got from my hypochondriac father had suddenly left me. I managed an undisturbed afternoon nap; and after routine pre-dinner visits from my internist and neurologist, I knew nothing more. Inquisitive to a fault though I'd been all my life, some deep-down voice was running me now. Its primal aim was self-preservation. *Don't make them tell you, and it may not happen. Whatever they tell you may be wrong anyhow. Stay quiet. Stay dark.*

In the evening I had my first CAT scan with a pleasantly jokey woman technician who gave no opinions; and I asked for none, though the core of my spine was displayed there on a screen before her. I was gambling that her levity meant that the images were good. I said to myself *They'll tell you in time.*

*

That proved to be at five o'clock the next afternoon; and the news unfolded decidedly on the staff's time, not mine. In the morning I'd had an unanesthetized hour of excruciating tests that required the insertion of large blunt-needle electrodes into the major nerves of my legs to measure the speed of motor impulses. Bad as it was, the hour provided my first acquaintance with the dry little knot of hospital pride that would be one of my few medical pleasures in coming months. However briefly, I could think *They may not have thrown the worst at you yet, but so far you've caught all their pitches.*

When the doctor who was measuring my nerve velocities learned that I was a writer, like so many laymen he deputized me an instant confessor. In a quiet hurry he all but told me his main secret. Something had bent his life nearly double several years ago—he got as far as saying he'd dropped out from medicine entirely and had returned only recently.

A seasoned listener, I dug no further but went on nodding.

Lately he'd come back from where he'd gone and had restarted here, this small clean lab. But for whatever reasons, he stopped his personal story there—he was a big-framed gentle creature. One final time he gouged his metal probes into my cringing long leg-nerves and said "You're tough. Just yesterday we had a professional football player in here for this, and he had to be led out screaming after thirty seconds."

By now the playground-dud buried in me was forced to smile.

The conclusive test was a myelogram, another thoroughly uncomfortable study involving the injection of an opaque dye into my spinal fluid, followed by a set of X rays down the length of my cord. It was less gruesome than the nerve-speed probes; but it added weight to my growing sense of being consumed by a single vast live idiot creature concealed throughout this enormous building. The creature had just one blank eye of the keenest focus and not one atom of self-awareness or even remorse at its endlessly accumulating knowledge, its power over the building's inhabitants—sick and well— and its impotence or refusal to help them.

At five o'clock on that second day, I was lying on a stretcher in a crowded hallway, wearing only one of those backless hip-length gowns designed by the standard medical-warehouse sadist. Like all such wearers I was passed and stared at by the usual throng of stunned pedestrians who swarm hospitals round the world.

My brother Bill Price was standing beside me, trying as ever to lift the tone with continuous jokes—a trait of our mother's; our brilliantly comic father would have been lugubrious here.

I was keeping up my lifelong role, straight man to his quips, when we saw my two original doctors bound our way with a chart in hand.

The initial internist would show his concern through years to come; but all I recall the two men saying that instant, then and there in the hallway mob scene, was "The upper ten or twelve inches of your spinal cord have swelled and are crowding the available space. The cause could be a tumor, a large cyst or something else. We recommend immediate surgery." I could hear they were betting on a long tumor, though I'd never heard of a tumor inside the cord itself. They mentioned the name of a young staff neurosurgeon they admired, and they suggested I go back to my room and await his visit.

Then they moved on, leaving me and my brother empty as wind socks, stared at by strangers.

As a member of the last American generation reared by the old-time family doctor of endless accessibility and tact, I'll have later chances here to expand on the well-known but endlessly deplorable and faceless—sometimes near-criminal—nature of so much current medicine. For now I'll flag a single question, familiar to millions in similar corners. What would those two splendidly trained men have lost if they'd waited to play their trump till I was back in the private room for which Blue Cross was paying our mutual employer, Duke, a sizable mint in my behalf?

At least on private ground, with the door shut, the inevitable shock of awful news could have been absorbed, apart from the eyes of alien gawkers, by the only two human beings involved. It might have taken the doctors five minutes longer; and minutes are scarce, I understand, in their crowded days. I also know that for doctors who work, from dawn to night, in the same drab halls, it all no doubt feels like one room. But any patient can tell them it's not, and I've often wondered how many other such devastating messages they bore that day to actual humans as thoroughly unready as I for the news.

The neurosurgeon entered my room a half hour later. He was Allan Friedman, then a small-bodied man in his early to mid-thirties with mad-scientist spectacles, a full mustache and a square jaw. My mother had undergone brain surgery at Duke Hospital in 1963; so I was familiar with the general staff attitude toward neurosurgeons—that they're the most brilliant, most heavily pressed and difficult of that strange band who've made the choice to spend their adult lives cutting people. And at first sight Friedman did look a little extraplanetary, largely because of his thick glasses and intensely grave demeanor.

I'd experience his attentive concern in years to come;

14

but at first sight I only thought in bold colors, *He's alarmingly young, at least fifteen years my junior; but that may be good—his hands will be steady.* I also thought that his youth might link him with the test-pilot daring which characterized American neurosurgeons of earlier days. And in fact early in our first meeting, Friedman distinguished himself from those older heroes by saying that neurosurgeons now tended to be a good deal more restrained in approaching organs as fragile as the brain and spinal cord. He said in effect that the old-timers loved "heroic procedures," going in and tearing out an alien presence, however devastating to the patient; current surgeons were more cautious.

But first he sat with me and Bill and gave us his version of my possibilities. There seemed to be something foreign within my upper spine—the normal cord is roughly the size of an adult thumb. The thing inside me had put a sizable kink in my vertebrae, a curve that might well explain my lost height. Worse, it had swollen the volume of my cord till the cord was crowding the hollow canal through the vertebrae.

That crowding resulted inevitably in a compression of the thousands of so-far-irreparable nerve fibers that make the cord such a vital but vulnerable cable. The crowding had probably, for months or years, developed slowly enough for my cord and brain to accommodate the pressure. But lately they'd run out of dodges and detours. That would explain the relatively sudden rush of symptoms after healthy-seeming decades. Our best hope would be for a large cyst that could be surgically drained and permanently shunted. A worse case would be a benign tumor that might or might not lend itself to harmless extraction. Successful removal would depend upon whether the tumor was self-encapsulated within the spinal tissue or

15

had infiltrated the tissue so intricately that it couldn't be dissected without my death or total paralysis.

The worst case would be an infiltrating tumor which proved malignant. No further external procedures could tell us much more about the problem. The magnetic resonance imager or MRI, so useful now in soft-tissue studies, would not reach most American hospitals for another few months. Having laid out that bill of particulars, Friedman recommended immediate surgery. This was late Thursday afternoon; his Friday schedule was filled—on Monday morning then.

I remember asking "What if I decline surgery?"

He said my symptoms would rapidly worsen. He didn't elaborate.

As a child-veteran of the polio epidemics of the 1940s—one who'd visited an iron-lung ward with its rows of trapped children whose lungs were paralyzed—I understood that the nerves controlling my lungs and diaphragm would likely be next to surrender to the pressure. I was only beginning to realize that all my doctors had now entered their laconic "Tell-him-nothing-he-doesn't-ask-for" mode, but I doubt I asked another question—no fishing for predictions or probabilities. My buried censor was guarding me still against news I couldn't handle at present.

With the keen sympathy of our forty-three years together, through thick and thin, Bill likewise asked nothing.

Since I was in one of the world's major hospitals—one in which I'd be treated by my university colleagues and where virtually all my expenses would be paid by the generous insurance policy provided by an unusually benign employer—I never considered taking second opinions. I turned to Bill and said "There's no choice."

A veteran of Vietnam and the Navy, Bill had always made quick decisions like mine, for good or bad. He nodded now and said "Apparently." It was another trait we'd learned from our mother, an instinctive quick-mover; our father would agonize for months at the simplest pair of options.

I also know that at the moment I could recall our half-blind mother's voice, long years ago, in this same hospital. After days of primitive and excruciating tests in an effort to find the cause of her blindness, a blunderbuss neurologist had loudly told me at her open room-door, "It's the worst thing it could possibly be—two large aneurysms deep in her brain."

When I'd gone in to her moments later with a gentler version, she'd borne it strongly with a single nod—"All my life I've been the Jonah" (the single passenger thrown overboard at the height of a storm to save the ship, then caught and trapped in a whale's dark belly).

Was I the family's next stunned Jonah? There was no time to think.

Friedman was on his feet to leave, silent and staring.

I told him to make plans for Monday morning.

A moment after he left the room and shut the door, I heard a firm knock. It was Dorothy Roberts, a friend of long standing and of wolf-den loyalty. She also worked in the English Department, we'd been sworn friends for three decades, and now she'd brought me a stack of the day's mail. I'd stood with her through two removals of ruptured discs in this same place a few years back, and the sight of her great dark eyes at this moment caved me in. I was with two people I trusted as much as anyone alive; they'd never done me the slightest harm. For the first time yet, I broke down and wept.

Bill and Dot stayed near till I calmed a minute later,

17

and then we laid out the little we knew like a stockade around us against the unknown. Neither one of them stooped to sham consolations. What they had to give was their honest presence; and while that constituted a lot, soon I asked them to let me be. If I was going to fold up again, I'd do it on my own time.

Once they'd left I ate a cold supper and spent the evening in the dark watching a televised documentary on the history of the ballet *Giselle*. I don't recall indulging in any hard fear or deep soul-searching. Doubtless I prayed for God's will to be worked, and I'm sure I added the usual clear postscript reminding him of my wishes in the matter—he mustn't act on an insufficient sense of my needs. This much though is sure from that night; before I slept I wrote another poem in the daybook.

> *At five p.m., grim as Charon's punt,*
> *The neurologist finds me on my stretcher by the door*
> *Of the radiological torture-tank*
> *In which four searchers kind as children*
> *Have found the fault—"A ten-inch tumor*
> *On your spinal cord."*
> *   Now at nine*
> *I lie here alone, flanked by chatter and howls,*
> *And watch TV—a flabby endless*
> *Documentary "Portrait of Giselle,"*
> *Starring Anton Dolin with clips of Markova,*
> *Alonso, Makarova: each her own*
> *Absurd self blazed by white elation,*
> *Cause of the helpless joy I sport*
> *In this hot stale proliferating dark.*

My hands had been coached since early childhood by excellent teachers to attempt such fending at the first sign of threat.

And Saturday morning I managed a final entry before the surgical pause.

> *My name is* Edward Reynolds Price,
> *So here on the ward I'm* Edward Price.
>
> *Last night I looked at my new neighbor's door.*
> *He's* Edward Reynolds, *plain as ink.*
>
> *Which one of us is the other's* doppelgänger?
> *Scapegoat? Porter of an alternate fate?*

Later that Saturday I was rolled back to radiology for arteriograms, X-ray studies of my spinal arteries. Friedman wanted as full a sense as possible of the terrain he was about to enter. Twenty-one years ago arteriograms had been the test that diagnosed my mother's aneurysms. They'd also nearly killed her with pain, shock and violent nausea—the only event in her life she told me she'd never willingly repeat. I mentioned that memory to the same technicians who'd managed the myelogram on Friday, and they assured me that the opaque dyes had been greatly improved in two decades and were much less toxic. I should only feel a brief slight burning.

The test was brief but hardly slight. As the dye jetted into my right arm, I could follow its scalding path through my chest, up into my brain, down my spine— with a pause at my butthole—then out both legs. I never asked the cheerful technicians if they learned any news, and they told me none.

But the young presiding radiologist followed my stretcher out and said he was sorry to have been the one to find my trouble. His kindness was startling in its newness; and before I could thank him, he added a sentence I've often recalled. "See, at first I thought you had something even worse than this."

I asked him what.

He said "M.S."—multiple sclerosis.

For what it was worth at that bleak point, I knew that my early fear had been realistic; and the laughing atmosphere of the X-ray tank gave me a brief whiff of hope that now I'd entered some big joint effort to rescue my spinal cord and legs—the kind of World War II alliance I'd known as a boy, to stop the marauder and reclaim lost ground.

After the hot arteriograms there was little to do but wait out a long spring weekend, talking with visitors, calling more friends, searching the unlikely hospital air and the faces of busy nurses and interns for favorable omens. Again I'm sure I must have prayed. Since adolescence, short and long prayers have seldom failed to be a reflex for me. In fear or pleasure I generally find myself saying "Over to you; your will be done."

But I don't recall any special tack from that long weekend or any deals I offered to cut with God in return for life or the movement of my four limbs or the use of my lungs. Maybe I was allowing, barely allowing, for the kind of last-moment rescue I'd known more than once from childhood convulsions and bronchial seizures. I was old enough to believe in catastrophe, but I wouldn't beckon it onward toward me.

Strangely I don't recall dread either, though since shortly after my father's terrible death from lung cancer three decades before, I'd had several bouts of cancer phobia. I'd grow convinced that a lump or spot I'd newly discovered was oncoming death, and I'd often refuse to trust the doctors who'd tell me the little knot in my side or chest was benign. I'd insist on tests that, till now, had always confirmed the doctor's opinion—nothing there, I was safe. In retrospect, surely the tests had been inadequate.

Now I almost surely wasn't safe. A tumor was almost surely in me at last. Hadn't my unconscious mind long ago detected its alien presence and tried to warn me in general terms through all these years—terms that had proved unconfirmable till now and had lulled me falsely? Why had I refused to pursue the warnings and make earlier doctors search even harder? Were we all too late now? And wasn't the only present question *Can the tumor come out and leave me alive?* Maybe I should have been stiff with apprehension, but the weight of Allan Friedman's answer last Friday in response to my only question—my surgical risks were death or quadriplegia—had stunned my mind into silent patience.

I remember the Sunday afternoon in hard detail. It was hot and dry, a fine green June 3rd; and Friedman had said I could visit home if I'd be back by five o'clock. Bill and Pia, my sister-in-law, had driven the twenty-five miles from Raleigh to get me. I walked out in street clothes with them for the six-minute ride to my house, which lay in open country.

On the way neither Bill nor I spoke of the parallel; but both of us thought of another Sunday, in February '54, when our father's surgeon gave him permission to leave the hospital and visit our home before they explored his lung Monday morning. The lung proved to be chocked with cancer; and though they removed it, Father died six days later, suffocated.

At my house Pia made coffee; and the three of us sat and tried to mimic a normal visit with the teasing games of raillery we'd played so well for years, concealing both our care and our mild normal family resentments. But after an hour the strain was too great. I took a wobbly look upstairs in my bedroom at the wall of pictures of friends and loves I'd assembled to face me, morning and night; these reminders of their presence had been both a source of delight and a good wailing-wall for years now—they could listen mutely.

And since I'd notified all those friends who were still alive, I thought I could sense their hope like a firm wind at my back. It felt like the pressure of transmitted courage, sent from as far off as Britain and Africa; and that was the thing I needed most now—that and the effort to string a usable line of communication with what I call God. Even a person who lacks any sense of a watchful creator may be excused in a storm for grasping at whatever looks remotely like help, and I've never known a full hour of doubt that I was made and watched by the single source of all life.

What I hadn't felt, except for that brief breakup on Friday, was real self-pity. The odds, however badly skewed, seemed beatable still, though as we drove away from the house again in late afternoon, I couldn't help trying to burn certain sights deep into my mind—the old beech trees with trunks the color and shape of elephant legs, the pond that for so many years had harbored a particular great blue heron, the house itself that had sheltered me and my friends for nineteen years. When we'd driven our father back to Rex Hospital after his visit home before surgery, he never saw any of it again—neither the place nor his younger son Bill nor his wife nor me, except through the haze of a drugged last agony.

I was back on the ward by five o'clock—Bill would join me again at dawn—and soon Friedman entered with the formal release for surgery. Again he had the duty to repeat his earlier warning of the risk of death or total paralysis, and he didn't attempt to couch his errand in any attempt at consolation. There's presumably no way to make such a moment palatable; and he didn't try, which was just as well. It may even have been on that same visit that he gave the first of several welcome openings onto who he was. At about that time anyhow he told me "I'm the kind of guy who goes to a convention of neurosurgeons in Geneva; and when all the others head out to dinner, I wind up in the nearest library, reading case studies."

I appreciated his bald candor that Sunday afternoon; and since he looked grimmer than I felt, I obeyed an impulse to cheer him up with a recent joke.

He gave me the first grin I'd seen on him; but it faded fast as it always would—young as he was, he'd seen a great deal of pain.

Then I signed his release with what flair I could muster. As I watched his back leave the room however, I told myself *You've put your life in the hands of a boy young enough to be your son.*

I spent the rest of a dinnerless evening in another small lab with a likable young woman who performed a set of evoked-potential tests on my relevant nerve tracts. They were less painful than the earlier leg-velocity tests; and since I'd been given a mild sedative, they proved an oddly peaceful diversion. By the time they were done, I was tired and—after more phone calls to and from friends—I slept with no trouble till a while before dawn when Bill walked in, then Jeff Anderson just back from his honeymoon; and shortly behind them at 6:15, the regulation two men in loose green suits with a stretcher.

What I mainly saw though was an earlier dawn when Bill and I had joined our mother before her brain surgery. Bad as we felt when we entered the room, she was upright on pillows with a scarf round her head. At the sight of us, she tore off the scarf, revealing her newly shaved bare skull and exclaiming "Khrushchev!"—the Russian leader then, as bald as she. Then she laughed and said "Please finish the Twenty-third Psalm for me." She'd tried all night to get past "He leadeth me beside still waters."

It would be my first surgery since I lost my tonsils at eighteen months, and the thought of a long anesthetized day at the mercy of knives weighed on me more than the prospect of death or paralysis. All through childhood I'd heard adults describe the effects they'd suffered from ether—clanging noises, sirens and bells, nightmares and the urge to babble secrets. So I won't claim to being eager to lay myself on the narrow stretcher and have a white sheet pulled up to my chin, but I felt as ready as I'd ever be for such an uncontrollable venture, and I moved on my own steam through the short gap from bed to stretcher.

The stretcher bearers reminded me to remove my ring, a black onyx my father had given me when I was nineteen. And for a moment I recalled that for years a simple holograph will had lurked inside my desk at home. I'd made no attempt to update it in the midst of this crisis. It was too late now to do more than take off the ring, the small chain with a cross, and my spectacles. I held them out to Jeff for safekeeping.

The glasses slipped between our hands and cracked on the floor—an omen of course, however we tried to dismiss it with laughter.

By the time we'd passed a few smiling nurses and were on the elevator bound up, the Martian unreality of blue-lit sterile surgical space enfolded me deeper with each set of doors. And when Bill bent to kiss my forehead at the final doors, saying he'd see me the moment I woke, I was gliding at the end of a very long tether, farther out than I'd ever been from my body or mind and entirely at ease (a bedtime dose of Valium, the first of my life, may still have been active).

A ring of surgical technicians closed in around me, low-keyed and undiscourageable as dwarves in a tale; and quickly I was calmer still as they busied themselves with intravenous needles and wrappings. Friedman seemed to be nowhere near. I only recall the anesthetist, a smiling young woman, down near my eyes.

She said "Do you like the taste of garlic?"

I nodded Yes.

She said "Then here comes a taste of garlic." Her hand moved toward the needle in my arm.

A taste of wild onions, not garlic, shot past my throat. I had an instant to say "It's *onions*," then was totally gone.

Through the next ten hours, there was never a thought or hint of consciousness, no dreams or family secrets divulged (so far as I've heard). Then after a timeless day at the will of a squad of strangers—each capable of ending my life with incompetence, an honest mistake or malice—I swam up slowly in a different light to the voices of a man and two women above me.

"Mr. Price, wake up." Their hands were on me. "Do you know where you are?"

I said "I hope I'm in Duke Hospital."

One of the women with a round black face said "Got it first pop!"

I asked the time.

"Five-thirty p.m."

I was still too groggy to calculate that I'd been gone a whole spring day, but I guessed I was living anyhow. My mind requested my right arm to move. It lurched up, stabilized and hung firm before me. I asked the fingers to move; and they did, strong and free. The left hand likewise. But I asked the attendants no more questions. *Stay low. You'll know when you need to know.*

And when I tried to crane up and see the space around me—a huge plain covered with fog the color of cream— the nurses pressed me back and said we were bound any minute for Intensive Care.

I recalled our first sight of Mother back in Intensive Care from her own long day of unconscious waiting while a few men cut deep into her forebrain. As her eyes caught us, she'd said "When are they going to operate?" The long ordeal, which had barely helped her, still seemed an impending threat.

Now at least I knew I'd cleared one hurdle. I know I even tried to think it would prove the last.

It was only in Intensive Care, after Bill had spent awhile feeding me the crushed ice I craved, that the anesthesia wore off enough to let me sense the start of pain that would be my constant companion till now. Though it would grow and diversify with time, it declared its nature and shape that evening. I can still call back that first awareness, the clear sense of a white-hot branding iron in the shape of the capital letter "I" held against my upper spine from the hairline downward some ten or twelve inches and unrelenting.

It would be years to come before Duke Hospital entrusted morphine pumps to its patients, and soon I was asking the splendid nurses for most of the help they were licensed to give. In all my eventual hospital time, I never encountered better nurses than the no-nonsense yet merciful women who worked Intensive Care round the clock. They gave me morphine when orders permitted; so what I remember of that first night and the next two days was filtered through the dense but transparent screen of a powerful opiate, a treacherous friend.

I know that Bill told me at some point in the evening that Yes they'd found a large tumor, removed some of it and that Yes it was malignant though maybe of a slower rate of growth than Friedman had feared—the final pathology report was still pending. That first night's knowledge of just what I still harbored inside me was buffered so well by frequent morphine that I know my first thought was mild annoyance, couched in terms of the popular-mythical date for a cancer cure. *Damn, I'll have to wait five years till I know I'm cured.*

And that unreal state of ease prevailed through the next days, Tuesday and Wednesday in a new private room on the neurosurgical ward. Though I mostly stayed in bed, I met my colleagues and local friends with an aplomb they still laugh about. It seems I engaged in lucid personal and business conversations of which I have no memory whatever. All of me floated on the tranquil sea of suave morphine, the nearest chance of a live return to the carefree safety of the womb.

Friedman stopped by twice a day; and unlike most members of the senior staff in a teaching hospital, he never arrived with a guard of students. He came alone with his own intense focus; and I grew increasingly respectful of that, though still I resisted pressing for answers. I do recall that on the Tuesday morning when I was still drugged, Friedman repeated with new precision what Bill had told me the previous night.

The tumor was pencil-thick and gray-colored, ten inches long from my neck-hair downward and too intricately braided in the core of my spinal cord to permit him to do much more than sample its tissue in several places.

I could taste the depth of his disappointment, but I only asked a single question—how much of the tumor he'd actually removed.

He said "Maybe ten percent."

It was a further shock. I'd assumed that a whole day's surgery had achieved more than ten percent. That was hardly more than a biopsy sample.

Then he told me that initial pathology reports suggested a malignant astrocytoma or glioma, both of which are tumors arising from nerve tissue. He defined the word *malignant* as descriptive of tissue which grows without normal structure or control—I recall his saying with a kind of aesthetic frown that the cells "look wild and ugly" under a microscope. And he added that, while preliminary reports suggested that my tumor was not of the highest degree of malignancy, its presence was still a grave fact.

In lieu of significant tumor removal, he'd taken a sizable palliative step. He'd chiseled off a good deal of bone from seven vertebrae in my upper spine to decompress crowding in the area. Since chemotherapy had not yet shown impressive success in stemming tumors of the central nervous system, he recommended radiation once my long incision had healed—about a month from now. As a cold comfort he ended by saying that malignant tumors of the central nervous system seldom spread elsewhere in the body.

28

I remember thinking *The standard good news/bad news joke—congratulations, your brand of cancer likely won't spread; but we can't get it out of the main control room.*

It was not till Thursday when Friedman told me he was taking me off morphine, then and there, that the full force of the surgical news and its threat began to reach me. With every hour of time in the real world, minus morphine, I moved toward a single understanding. *This lethal eel is hid in my spinal cord and will kill me.* From early childhood I'd had a tendency to think in pictures more than in words. My thoughts are mostly silent movies, or wide still-pictures, behind my eyes. So once my mind was sober again, I quickly saw the threat as a thing, a visible object; and from the first that object was a dark gray eel embedded live in the midst of my spine.

The picture-making went on with a vengeance for the next three nights, force-feeding me all the omens and fears that the opiate had screened. On morphine I'd slept too deeply to dream. Now suddenly withdrawn, I felt the pain of both my wounds, to mind and body. On successive nights I responded by staging, for the first time in years, long credible nightmares. They were far more shapely and terrifying than any I could remember from childhood, and they plainly poured through me from the seed of cancer-dread.

The first night for instance I constructed a convincing tale of going alone to a Caribbean island for rest and pleasure. Once there and settled in, I discovered slowly through several days that my deluxe beach hotel—made entirely of spotless wickerwork and at which I was somehow the only guest—was staffed by real vampires who'd learned to tolerate the tropical sun. At first they were affable, charming me with perfect service but actually waiting till they'd lowered my caution and could drain me dry.

In the second night's dream I was lost in thick darkness and couldn't find home but wandered with increasing panic through a vicious landscape, balked at all turns. I'd wake and assure myself, then drop back off and be lost again.

The third night was worst, but that dream finally stated its point with brute candor. I was walking the seventy miles from Durham to Warren County, North Carolina to find my birthplace, my mother's home-place in the village of Macon. When I found the house and searched the rooms, it proved abandoned and sadly empty—no relation of mine had lived there for years. But once I was outside again in the dark, a small young black-haired man appeared like a cringing demon, writhing around me in a sinuous dance; then saying "Now you must learn the bat dance." I suddenly knew that his bat dance was death, death from cancer. Still dreaming, I summoned my strength to refuse him.

Weeks later I'd preserve that third nightmare in a poem that's faithful to the shape of the dream. It's called "The Dream of Refusal"; and it ends with the words that ended the night, a vow to myself.

I will walk all night. I will not die of cancer.
*Nothing will make me dance in that dark.**

From the moment I made that refusal, asleep, I'd begun anyhow to lean on the only visible prop that

---

* The whole poem is included here on page 198 in a group of poems relevant to the account of my experience.

couldn't quit me this side of death—my own self. Like a number of men of my generation, I'd missed the Second World War by some six years (I was twelve in 1945). With college deferments I'd likewise missed Korea; and in the various Berlin confrontations and Vietnam, no branch of the service had wanted me. As a writer who admired the war stories and novels of so many soldier-authors, I'd often wondered to what extent my apparent luck was in fact a deprivation.

Now at last I must enter what was plainly a war, with life-or-death stakes, and assume the fight in the only way I knew to fight—in the arts of picture-making and story-telling that I'd worked at since childhood. I'd be myself to the outer limit of all I could be, resourceful as any hunted man in the bone-dry desert, licking dew from cactus thorns. So even that early, I'd cast myself as the hero of an epic struggle, and I saw both the ludicrous melodrama of that role and the urgent need for it.

I stayed in the hospital three more weeks. Between the visits from friends and doctors, the start of physical therapy and the fitting for a chromium walker and a shiny quad cane (a cane with four feet for greater support), I managed occasional bouts of the blues as unprecedented symptoms arrived almost by the day. Numbness was spreading all down my right leg, then was taking the sole and toes of my left foot. My genitals were partly numb to one side of an invisible vertical line, ruthlessly drawn through their exact center.

And late in the afternoon each day, I'd be overwhelmed by a rising sense of dissociation from my whole body. My mind would seem to leak out, rise above my trunk and limbs and gaze down at them from a helpless nearness. *When can I live again in my body? And where am I now?* As much as any specter in a ghost tale, I felt like a spirit haunting the air above his old skin that had suddenly, and for no announced reason, evicted me and barred my return. More than once I felt even worse—like a butchered steer, hooked up in space above my old home.

When I'd describe each change as it came to Friedman on his twice-daily visits, he'd only say "That's a tumor sign" with blank assurance; and I'd ask no more. My instinct to hunker on in ignorance strengthened with every sight of a doctor. *Don't probe for news. News will sink you fast and—anyhow—what do they know?*

It would be a year before I knew that, aware of my tendency to fulfill forecasts, Bill Price wisely hadn't told me the word he'd got from Paul Bennett, our cousin by marriage and an excellent doctor. When Bill phoned Paul the night after my surgery, gave him Friedman's news from pathology and asked Paul flatly "What does this mean?", Paul had said "It means six months to paraplegia, six months to quadriplegia, six months to death."

Yet a few days after surgery, I was taking unaided short walks in the room and the hall outside. I was shaky, to be sure; but I needed no props. And I was still trusting that the pain would cool as the long incision healed and my shoulder muscles found new attachments to the hacked-on streamlined vertebrae. Those tentative hopes were braced by daily visits from my friends Keith Brodie and David Sabiston. Brodie was then a practicing staff psychiatrist; he would soon be president of the university. David Sabiston, then as now, was one of the world's great surgeons and a senior member of the hospital staff. Not only did their visits seem to win me small attentions from the ward staff, they half convinced me to believe their plainly expressed optimism. I recall for instance that Keith and Brenda Brodie gave me a small crystal ball "to contemplate your happy future" and that David Sabiston promised to be at my ninetieth birthday party; so I learned, late in life, that such homely offerings to the gravely ill can have a weight that even the giver may not foresee. They can quickly swell into amulets for health and hope, even in minds more rational than mine.

I also hoped in those hospital days, though a lot less strongly than I'd have guessed, that sexual desire would soon revive and reach outside me. Since childhood, sex had been an enormous motor for my life and work; and while the surgery might have left me impotent, it hadn't, despite the partial numbness. But from the moment I'd waked after surgery, the hunger to know and please other bodies was suddenly and inexplicably gone for the first time in nearly forty years. Was I merely still lulled from the hours of anesthesia (a doctor friend had already told me I'd feel its effects for at least a year)?

When I thought occasionally of the unprecedented and apparently uncomplicated absence of desire, I recalled the words of a friend who'd been a prisoner of the Germans near the end of the Second War. When I'd asked him about sexual activity in his camp, where men were barbed-wired off from the women, he quietly said "Once you're starving for actual food, sex is the last thing to cross your mind." Had some deep need of my life, a need that till now had been fed by sexual warmth, found other nourishment? Or was that need merely dazed and waiting? Would the strange departure of such a crucial component of my work kill or deform the work?

It would be months before I thought I knew answers to any such questions; and even now I'm not convinced that I understand how so powerful a force simply went underground, or became another kind of force, for the better part of six or seven years. In any case, I weathered the long abstinence with extremely few conscious or unconscious anxieties—I'm a good recaller of dreams, and from those years I recall no dreams that seem concerned with an absence of sex.

As in all hospitals, time bore down between events. For me it hung surprisingly heavy because, for the first time since grade school, I'd run head-on into a block on my work. Aside from the several daybook poems, I couldn't so much as think of resuming my novel *Kate Vaiden*. Any work as demanding as entry into whole other lives must wait till I was home. Stranger still, I found myself unable to read anything longer than a magazine article. My eyes were normal but my patience was gone. I couldn't sit still for a serious or even a frivolous book, not in my own hands.

But friends had already started bringing me joke books, cartoons, books full of pictures of peaceful sights, and detective novels. My friends at the video-rental store even arrived unexpectedly to hook up a tape player in my hospital room—to show me an assortment of Marx Brothers films—but their player proved incompatible with hospital wiring. The one exception to my book-and-movie famine centered on regular visits from a student friend, Yoji Yamaguchi.

Because he was taciturn and I was hardly eager to talk, I soon asked Yoji if he'd read aloud from *Robinson Crusoe*, which I'd brought in with me. Each afternoon then, he sat by the bed and read in his calm voice for half an hour while I mainly dozed in and out through Crusoe's tale of his own marooned life, his slow invention of tools for his alternate existence. It was days before I began to see the aptness of the book I'd grabbed at random the day I left home—a shipwrecked lone man inventing a life.

And I listened to music as if it were literally life-or-death food. Again I didn't examine the choices—they constituted a different fare from my usual listening—but later I saw clear patterns among the tapes I played so often on a small machine beside my bed. I couldn't for instance listen long to vocal music unless it was choral and coolly distant. No turbulent opera, no pleading egos, no dwelling on loss or grief or chaos. I couldn't even listen to the comic operas of Mozart and Rossini which had helped me through a number of earlier blue intervals. And I couldn't bear the company of any solo voice except the wide reach of Leontyne Price.

Her voice, as it had since the night I first heard it in New York in 1953 (the legendary revival of *Porgy and Bess* with William Warfield and Cab Calloway), offered glimpses of an ideal sphere of triumphant ease, all the more real because she was so indisputably already there as the voice spun on, in full description of a goal she'd reached ahead of me.

Mostly I listened to the high baroque orchestral masters. I'd spent my college and graduate career immersed in English baroque poetry, and I'd studied baroque sculpture and architecture on numerous visits to Rome; so the intricate complexities of the age, twining as they did round one central cause—the praise of God and his creation—had plainly met an old need in me to confirm the order which I'd always trusted was present behind confusion and chaos.

But now with a whole new appetite, I'd lie full-dressed on my bed and listen time and again to Gabrieli's canzone for brass, Cavalli's *Missa Concertata*, the four orchestral suites of Bach, Handel's august concerti grossi,

Albinoni's concerti, Vivaldi's *Gloria* (RV 589) and more. They were pieces I'd known for years, but now I was hearing them as if for the first clear time. I'd lie alone, as still as I could manage with both eyes shut, and concentrate on letting the actual visible line of the harmony enter my mind—coiling as baroque lines do, luxuriantly but in strict logic—till that line reached the core of my spine. Its lucid conclusion in benign order seemed to help me crowd out the idiot killer encysted in me, the blind eel bumbling toward my brain.

Odd as it seems looking back, though I saw the tumor in those terms, I never felt the horror of its presence that so many other cancer hosts describe. I hardly felt comfortable, feeling its large existence within me; but I was never driven, like others I've known, by a constant passion to tear its repulsive life from my body. Maybe again its long presence had let me accept it as a virtual twin (by now I felt deeply convinced of its presence in and with me since the womb, since conception).

I wonder now, though, if the steady presence of music around me didn't contribute importantly to my sense of the cancer as a thing with its own rights. Now it sounds a little cracked to describe, but then I often felt that the tumor was as much a part of me as my liver or lungs and could call for its needs of space and food. I only hoped that it wouldn't need all of me. In any case, along with the few short poems I was able to write in those early weeks, the music of others—heard as intently as if I'd made it—was the first big weapon in my battery of healing, my own campaign to outlast the eel. War started in earnest when I went home on June 22nd.

2

A WEEK LATER on June 30th I managed the first thing I'd written since surgery, a short poem recording the fact that, back in my house, I woke one morning with the taste of delicious dwarf Bartlett pears in my mind, the pears my father would bring me in childhood.

> *Perfect pears no bigger than hen eggs*
> *Gold, spotted brown, one mouthful even*
> *For me a boy. My father's brought them*
> *Home from a trip; and I devour*
> *Them in one long evening, then sleep*
> *Black dreamless night till he shakes me—Sunday,*
> *His day.*
>   *Forty-six years pass. Home*
> *From surgery (tumor still in me), I wake*
> *At dawn and taste that cool flesh;*
> *Hear his waking voice.*

His voice, I knew, was present only in memory; but I was ready at least to think that, wherever he was, he knew of me now and was pressing his old concern toward me.

By then I could walk unassisted for short stretches around the house; and with the cane I could make short tours round the yard. My gait was not a great deal worse than before the surgery, though my distance was strictly limited; but the growing numbness in legs and feet was steadily weakening my sense of balance. If you can't feel the ground through the soles of your shoes, you move in a dream and are likely to topple at the smallest obstruction.

The strange new sense of being suspended outside my body was also growing more frequent and lending my days an eerie unreality. The eeriness rose apparently from new failures in proprioception—that set of faculties which responds to the hundreds of sensations produced within us and tells us, without our conscious monitoring, where the various parts of our physical bodies lie in relation to one another. I'd rise from a chair and still feel seated for a curious moment till my mind caught up with the vertical action. And if I didn't watch my feet closely, I couldn't tell where they were planted from moment to moment. I would suddenly notice that my lower limbs were splayed or twisted at painful angles, except that now they gave me no pain—none beyond the burn in my back. There were compensations though.

My weight after weeks of hospital food was down to 155 pounds, my college weight. I could easily shower and dress myself. The pain that had burned in my back since surgery seemed at times to be cooling and fading. And home visits three days a week from a physical therapist pushed me to strengthen what little was left of nerve connection and muscle control in my shoulders, back, chest and legs.

My first therapist was Diana Betz, a woman who proved her loyalty in numerous professional and friendly acts of generosity and who played a tangible part in my survival. With never a trace of complacency, she quietly proved that a thoroughly skilled medical practitioner can give a patient constant human sympathy, frequent warm laughter and realistic caution without surrendering her own perspective and self-possession. I can add further that I was by no means the only patient of a private therapist with time on her hands—Diana invariably came to me at the end of long days spent full-time in the pediatric wards of Duke Hospital, often working with badly damaged infants and children.

For the first few days back home, one of several friends would drive out toward sundown, help me make a light supper; then stay for the night. I had no fear of being alone in an isolated house, but I was too shaky to cook for myself without the risk of burning numb flesh, and the chance of a fall that would tear my incision was considerable. Still I had no reason to think I wouldn't be on my own in a matter of days. Surely by the time I was set to begin radiation treatments on July 5th, I'd be firm enough on my pins to drive myself to the clinic. With my still undependable feet, I hadn't tried driving.

But I grew no firmer; and on the morning of July 3rd, I had the single strangest experience of my life till now. I've mentioned my tendency to pray, convinced as I am that my life is intended by a sometimes merciful power that's at least connected to, if not identical with, what I believe is the maker of all we know. My means of thinking about that power and its intentions were formed in my early childhood by the texts and rites of an unchurchly Christianity which was passed to me by my parents.

I've also been more or less constantly aware of the strong currents of impersonal force that have pressed against my thoughts since infancy and that still appear to

39

come from that creator, in outright gifts or in odd synchronicities of time and place that hint of a nearly plain meaning to life. The added fact that, in the 1970s, I'd spent months translating the Gospel of Mark surely helped to shape the experience of that July morning in '84. Mark's gospel is widely thought to be the oldest of four canonical gospels; and because of its focus on the startling acts of Jesus at the expense of his teaching, it's far the most vivid account of the imprint his short life made.

I'd slept the previous night alone in my house and had waked at daylight. I was propped on pillows against the head of my old brass bed. No lights were on but I was surely conscious—I'm an easy riser, clearheaded from the moment my eyes click open. I was thinking naturally of the past ordeal, the massive violence done to my body, and of all the unknowns that I'd only just learned might lie ahead.

I'd visited the radiation oncology clinic at Duke three times in the previous week. There I'd had my first chilling encounter with the radiologist who'd supervise my treatment. In two further visits I'd lain still for the lengthy making of a plaster cast of my shoulders and chest and then undergone a dry run of the assault on the tumor. That assault would involve my lying motionless on my chest in the cast for all my treatments, insured each time of lying in the same precise relation to an overhead X-ray beam. Small reference points were permanently tattooed on my back to insure exact focus on the tumor, and a long rectangle was outlined boldly in durable gentian-purple dye around my closed ugly scar.

The presiding radiation oncologist had begun our first meeting by telling me, with all the visible concern of a steel cheese-grater, that my tumor was of a size that was likely unprecedented in the annals of Duke Hospital—some fifty years of annals.

Maybe naturally I wondered *Does he want me to cheer with personal pride?*

Next he repeated, as a sole concession to hope, the news that spinal tumors rarely spread. Then he revealed that, in the interest of not simply arresting but fully destroying the tumor, I'd be given the maximum exposure then applied to the spinal cord—a total of some four thousand rads, given in increments five days a week for the next five weeks.

Though the oncologist never offered to tell me, I'd learned from my reading that one property of ionizing radiation is the disordering of genetic information in the nuclei of individual cells. An irradiated cell, in principle, is more likely than an unexposed cell to self-destruct when it attempts to divide and multiply. Since many malignant cells divide at considerably higher rates of speed than normal cells, radiation is likely to do greater damage to malignancies than to normal tissue, though it's by no means harmless to normal tissue. At best, maximal radiation therapy hopes to kill the tumor before the radiation itself kills or gravely damages the patient.

The oncologist did say, at our first meeting, that an absence of new symptoms for two years after radiation could be considered a cure. Though he didn't specify, I assumed that new symptoms for me would presumably involve further limits on walking, the use of my arms and control of my breathing. Then he ended with the kind of doctor's omen I was now too familiar with. If that large dose was given me, I'd bear a small but significant risk of losing the use of both my legs—say a five percent chance. I remember thinking *Don't tell me that; driven as*

I've always been to stand in the winner's circle, I'll surely land in the crippled five percent.

My friend Will Singer had accompanied me to the meeting. As we left, he acknowledged thinking the same thing—I shouldn't have been told of the five percent chance. My mind might take the chance and lunge.

So by daylight on July 3rd, morning thoughts of a stiff sobriety were plainly in order. But in the midst of such circular thinking, an actual happening intervened with no trace of warning. I was suddenly not propped in my brass bed or even contained in my familiar house. By the dim new, thoroughly credible light that rose around me, it was barely dawn; and I was lying fully dressed in modern street clothes on a slope by a lake I knew at once. It was the big lake of Kinnereth, the Sea of Galilee, in the north of Israel—green Galilee, the scene of Jesus' first teaching and healing. I'd paid the lake a second visit the previous October, a twelve-mile-long body of fish-stocked water in beautiful hills of grass, trees and small family farms.

Still sleeping around me on the misty ground were a number of men in the tunics and cloaks of first-century Palestine. I soon understood with no sense of surprise that the men were Jesus' twelve disciples and that he was nearby asleep among them. So I lay on a while in the early chill, looking west across the lake to Tiberias, a small low town, and north to the fishing villages of Capernaum and Bethsaida. I saw them as they were in the first century—stone huts with thatch-and-mud roofs, occasional low towers, the rising smoke of breakfast fires. The early light was a fine mix of tan and rose. It would be a fair day.

Then one of the sleeping men woke and stood.

I saw it was Jesus, bound toward me. He looked much

like the lean Jesus of Flemish paintings—tall with dark hair, unblemished skin and a self-possession both natural and imposing.

Again I felt no shock or fear. All this was normal human event; it was utterly clear to my normal eyes and was happening as surely as any event of my previous life. I lay and watched him walk on nearer.

Jesus bent and silently beckoned me to follow.

I knew to shuck off my trousers and jacket, then my shirt and shorts. Bare, I followed him.

He was wearing a twisted white cloth round his loins; otherwise he was bare and the color of ivory.

We waded out into cool lake water twenty feet from shore till we stood waist-deep.

I was in my body but was also watching my body from slightly upward and behind. I could see the purple dye on my back, the long rectangle that boxed my thriving tumor.

Jesus silently took up handfuls of water and poured them over my head and back till water ran down my puckered scar. Then he spoke once—"Your sins are forgiven"—and turned to shore again, done with me.

I came on behind him, thinking in standard greedy fashion, *It's not my sins I'm worried about.* So to Jesus' receding back, I had the gall to say "Am I also cured?"

He turned to face me, no sign of a smile, and finally said two words—"That too." Then he climbed from the water, not looking round, really done with me.

I followed him out and then, with no palpable seam in the texture of time or place, I was home again in my wide bed.

Was it a dream I gave myself in the midst of a catnap, thinking I was awake? Was it a vision of the sort accorded from a maybe external source to mystics of differing degrees of sanity through human history? From the moment my mind was back in my own room, no more than seconds after I'd left it, I've believed that the event was an external gift, however brief, of an alternate time and space in which to live through a crucial act.

For me the clearest support for that conclusion survives on paper in my handwriting. I've mentioned the sparseness of my calendar notes—hard happenings only, not thoughts or speculations. And in my calendar for '84, at the top of the space for Tuesday, July 3rd, I've drawn a small star and written

6 a.m.—By Kinnereth, the bath, "Your sins are forgiven" —"Am I cured?" —"That too."

I remain as aware as anyone of the highly suspect sound of my claim, but it's the only guess that seems to cover the hard facts. Above all, the event had a concrete visual and tactile reality unlike any sleeping or waking dream I've known or heard of, and it betrayed none of the surreal logic or the jerked-about plot of an actual dream. Even more convincingly, if it was a dream constructed by my mind to strengthen itself on the verge of an undertaking as destructive as five weeks of ionizing radiation—and since I was later to undergo even more daunting ventures on my body—then why did my mind never again award me a similar consolation in greater crises?

My later needs, in stretches of terror and deep depression, were more intense. But the plain fact is that I've never since known a remotely similar experience; nor again, had I ever before known anything similar in five decades of a life rich in fantasy and longing. Aside from the vision's astonishing newness and promise in the present condition of a man fifty-one years old who'd spent a good deal of his time in making and recording stories, it also became at once a piece of my history—a straightforward stretch of time lived through and confided to memory. And it confirmed two old convictions.

The first was my belief that the man Jesus, whose life and acts are reliably attested in more detail than those of Socrates or Julius Caesar, bore a mysterious relation to the creator. Whatever its nature, and my sense is that it included some form of identity, it was a close relation which I'd long since concluded was unique in the history of human experience known to me. My second conviction was a powerful suspicion that the creator takes close note of some creatures and apparently very little of others—a notice that's hardly egalitarian and that hardly always proves fortunate for the chosen creature or tribe, not if absence of pain is our unit of measure. The creator's *chosen* die so often in torment.

With those convictions then, if I was to take the morning in Kinnereth as a real event, I'd apparently been told that I was cured. Though Jesus' final words, "That too," had been pressed from him at my insistence, he'd nonetheless given them. In the bad times that log-jammed around me in the next three years, there'd be many days when fear and pain led me to doubt the reality of that morning by Lake Kinnereth—a kindly literary dream. There was even a night a few weeks later when, in a fiendishly convincing nightmare, my mind worked to prove to itself that my "vision" was a black satanic fraud. My unconscious strained mightily to convince me that the words and sights of the "vision" were manufactured with fiendish cunning from Nazi propaganda and were somehow planted in me by Joseph Goebbels, Hitler's master liar and a horror-comic feature in my childhood gallery of the ultimate villains in the Second War.

Yet through all the assaults I mounted on such an unprecedented and suspicious assurance, I was never quite able for two consecutive days to destroy the unassailably physical core of that morning—the credible acts that I'd watched, felt and heard in what was an actual place on Earth, a place I'd visited and photographed. That hard integrity clung to the memory; what it promised would somehow result in my body. So it did but by no means at once.

There were still the five weeks of X ray to face, twenty-five sessions on into August. Through the first two weeks, one of several friends drove me in at one o'clock. With a permit given only to radiation patients, we'd park in front of the oncology building. Then I'd have to navigate, on foot, some forty yards of distance to the waiting room. How I managed that walk became the first clearly visible daily gauge of my progress or loss. I'd check in briefly with a male secretary who kept me posted on my daily horoscope; then I'd leave my companion watching soap operas on the waiting-room TV and enter a lab for the day's quick and clean-seeming treatment. I'd lie face down in my body cast; the female technician would set up the tailor-made lead blocks to shield my good tissue, then she'd aim the beam precisely at the target range of my spine and leave the room. I'd hear a few seconds of sizzling above me (I seem to recall counting slowly to twenty); and with my eyes shut I'd imagine intensely a curative hand laid over my wound, the hand that had bathed me in Lake Kinnereth.

Back home, always exhausted from the body's fight against both the tumor and the lethal treatment, I'd sleep a good part of the afternoon. Then I'd eat a supper that Jeff and Lettie brought me; then I'd watch old video films till bedtime. Most of the first nights, I stayed alone in my bedroom and with no real concern. I could move round the house on my own steam, though shakily. I could tell myself *I'm on the mend now; we're doing something.*

Then just as new trouble came into view, I was joined by an old friend, Laird Ellis, who came from Florida to keep house for me while his wife and children were visiting in France. His daughter Katherine, then twelve, had been a great happiness for me in her childhood; and her injury a few months earlier in the bloody collision of her bicycle with an automobile had shaken me more than anything near me for several years. Laird cooked us good big meals, drove me in for the daily treatments, took long runs of his own in the afternoons, then sat with me through the evenings to watch the televised summer Olympics from Los Angeles. Though hopeless as an athlete, I've always respected the high pitch of natural gift and skill deployed in track and field and swimming, those acts involving the human body unadorned by pads or implements and pressed to excel in strength and grace.

Laird's presence was not just a practical help; he was also the second sane human being to say, flat-out and credibly, that he had no doubt I was going to survive (the first was Jeff Anderson). And the fact that Laird and I had spent little time together for years—and yet he was giving me this large service in expectation of no return—was a paradox that seemed like one firm patch of ground I could stand on till I was readier to take what came, from within and out.

So the underpinning of live support was holding beneath me, holding and strengthening by the week. I had no lack of volunteer company; near-strangers turned up with ready-cooked meals. My colleague Carl Anderson visited regularly, with campus mail and news, calmly affirming my continuance in a now distant-seeming job. And the chairman of my department—George Williams, who'd first remarked my changing gait—looked in on me often and was staunchly assuring about my place in the university. It was waiting for me; and if this trouble prolonged itself, I could easily shift to temporary disability payments that would match my salary. Meanwhile, as I've said, the university's excellent medical insurance was paying my mountainous bills for surgery, radiation, medicines and physical therapy.

A further help was my daily realization that, among my visitors and the random faces I'd meet in occasional visits with my shiny cane to a restaurant or store, I never once saw the open revulsion that so many cancer patients report. I watched but never saw a frown, no one ever flinched visibly at my approach, no one ever pulled back from a handshake. If anyone felt I was somehow contagious or awful to watch, they hid it well and have gone on hiding it.

Better still, the first week of radiation seemed nowhere near as hard as I expected. What could be less demanding than a therapy that consists, Monday through Friday (the tumor was given its weekends off), of walking on your own steam into an uncluttered room and lying still for under thirty seconds of exposure to an invisible beam—no apparent heat, no smell of burning, no detectable contact? At first the only significant aftermath was the profound exhaustion I've mentioned, though even the exhaustion was advertised to me by technicians as a sign that the rays were effectively killing the tumor (no one mentioned it was also killing me).

Admittedly the visible surroundings of the clinic were hardly encouraging. Despite alert nurses with plates of cookies, the upbeat ochre-colored walls and the astrological secretary, nothing could muffle the forbidding sight of the men and women in the small waiting room. Their varying states of emaciation and the look of their skin— blue, ashen or jaundiced—were only heightened by our efforts at a whispered mutual cheer among us. We tended to offer each other box scores—*I've only got six treatments to go; then I'm done for life. How about you?* And once a week I'd take the elevator upstairs to another lab where blood was drawn to monitor the treatment's effect on my white-cell count (white cells being main components of the body's immune system). Since the blood lab served all kinds of cancer patients, not simply those in radiation, its waiting room was gloomier than the one downstairs—crowds of men and women with the skeletal thinness and bald skulls of chemotherapy.

Always, in any part of the building, the hardest patients to meet were children, numerous and brave as blowtorches. Most awesome of all, in a long procession, was the monster-headed boy in a stroller who smilingly took his daily radiation just before me. A diffuse brain tumor and the treatments he got had swollen his head to bucket size, with knobs and knots in his dark purple skin. But he sat in his stroller with the well-earned swagger of a king's dwarf jester, maybe three years old, unable to speak.

Nor did any other human in view in the radiation oncology department, however well-meaning, reach me with any words that proved useful. A pair who tried valiantly were two of the ward's stretcher bearers, both women. In those weeks they were firmly committed to keeping me posted on the resignation of that year's Miss America who'd just been embarrassed by the publication of nude pictures of herself and was forced to resign. None of that news, nor any other, managed to mitigate my quick discovery that in my case at least, the most grueling treatment (one of the two most grueling brands of cancer treatment) would be presided over by a radiation oncologist—a medical doctor in his mid-thirties—who gave the unbroken impression, over five weeks, of being nothing so much as a nuclear physicist whose experimental subjects were, sadly for them, human beings.

With the second week though, I started to learn what was happening to me and the waiting others—I was being burned, good flesh and bad. For the first few days, I'd managed to joke that I was going to Hiroshima every day for lunch. Then once Friedman learned of my rapidly swelling legs and ankles, the spreading numbness and weakness and rising pain down my trunk and legs, he gave me his usual laconic description, "Radiation is not a benign therapy." I heard it as one of the drastic understatements of my life. He also said that the staff had concluded, on the basis of my tumor slides and the final report from a distinguished neuropathologist at the University of Virginia, that I was host to "a very bad tumor."

Again I asked for no details of its badness or speed—they might be wrong; I'd obey them if they told me—but I met his eyes dead-on and said "Allan, do I need to start making plans yet?" I didn't say for what.

He said "Not yet."

I said "But you'll tell me?"

He nodded once.

So the only medical hope for extending my present life was this assault by invisible rays of mindlessly unselective destruction on a narrow strip of my upper body where the tumor hid. My mouth and esophagus lay there as well, plus a stretch of my lungs and a good deal of other healthy tissue, including bone marrow (where immune cells are made) and whatever cells of my blood and lymph were flowing past in the moments of exposure. And all I could do—I or any of the baffled children and adults beside me—was endure the mystery and the radical damage with whatever help I could scrounge with my own hands.

In the midst of that second week, contact between my brain and my legs took another downward jolt. The trip from car to waiting room was harder each day, but I refused a wheelchair. The oncologist suspected that the new symptoms were the result of internal swelling in the cord, a natural response to destruction of the tumor. To reduce that inflammation, he started me back on dexamethasone (Decadron), the powerful steroid I'd taken for a few days before and after surgery. Through two months of heavy doses to come, it would prove another vicious deceiver; but—buffered by yet another pill, cimetidine (Tagamet) to prevent stomach ulcers—it acted fast.

One day after returning to drugs, I managed a startling number of leg lifts in physical therapy; and that night I could write in the calendar,

Feeling dramatically stronger. Walking, at home, without a cane. Best day since leaving hospital.

And I read another development as promising. In my first interviews at radiation, I'd been warned that the X ray might blister my esophagus and trachea and leave me temporarily unable to swallow solid food or speak, in which case I'd live on milkshakes and juices and communicate by writing. When that threat failed to materialize, I added one escape to my list of hopeful signs.

Despite my steadily weakening legs then, and the sudden fact that one morning all the bristles of my beard from lower lip to Adam's apple came out by the root and disappeared at the touch of my razor, I notched no further symptoms on the calendar. Laird and I went on spending quiet days with him reading and running and me doing little more than eating the prescribed high-protein meals to feed my immensely increased appetite and to counteract the rapid destruction of both benign and malignant tissue. So real was the destruction incidentally that, though I added protein powder to every meal and more than tripled my intake of calories, I gained no weight in the entire span. I likewise never suffered nausea, not once.

Toward the end of July, after two months of idleness at the panicky mercy of a strong steroid and at the urging of a helpful psychologist who talked with me several times about strategies for moving out of trauma into action, I managed to write one short group of poems, all addressed to my mother and called "The Eel." The roughly made poems elaborated, with all the bizarre thoughts of the time, my instinctive first image of the tumor as an alien and deadly eel concealed in my cord. One of the poems imagined clearly what I'd be if the eel won its fight; but they ended with the further statement of a hope that still seemed realistic or at least not foolish:

> To fight this hardest battle now—
> A man upright and free to give,
> In desperate need.*

---

* "The Eel" appears on page 200.

Still I had no thought of returning to my novel; I could barely make myself enter the study, and the sight of my computer was literally repellent. Even serious reading, my indispensable companion for years, continued to try my patience intolerably. Something in me was still deeply jangled or was focused intently on more urgent chores and makeshift pastimes. And despite the swarms of offered food and company from dozens of freehanded acquaintances, I was now avoiding visits from anyone but calm close kin and proven friends who'd ask me few questions, give no predictions and make no demands. To some acquaintances, my closing-down seemed thankless of me.

Many of them, I later discovered, read the seclusion as a sign that death was imminent and that I'd turned my face to the wall in despair. I was, to be sure, in a stunned condition; and there were long hours of melancholy when I tried to find which writers and other artists had died as young as fifty-one. Gustav Mahler seemed the prime example. Beethoven, a fellow bachelor, reached fifty-six and died shaking his fist at the sky. Among novelists, I found, middle age had often proved lethal (Dickens, Stendhal, Flaubert and Proust), though seldom as deadly as youth had proved for lyric poets and for Mozart and Schubert.

But with all the morbidity of such parlor games, some vital impulse spared my needing to reiterate the world's most frequent and pointless question in the face of disaster—*Why? Why me?* I never asked it; the only answer is of course *Why not?* And a lifetime's exposure to the rocky luck of my large family had innoculated me against the need to make an equally frequent claim—that my fate was unfair or unjust. Aware of the troubles of so many likable kinsmen around me in childhood and youth, I'd almost never expected fairness.

I'd likewise never shared the romantic indulgence of Dostoevsky's Ivan Karamazov who declares himself unable to yield to a God who demands or condones human suffering. From my pained but hilarious and magnanimous parents, I'd half understood that a normal life is sacrificial and is lived in good part, as in their case, for the sake of others or somehow for the unknown. This patch of fate I was treading now surely felt like sacrifice, though I often wondered for whom or what. In prayer I even occasionally tried to offer my trials in substitute for certain others whom I valued and saw in serious pain of their own, but a victim needs to be braver than I to take much comfort from that thin gruel—thin and mysterious (you'll never know if your pain is credited to another's account).

My other means of what felt like prayer, in the wake of the vision and my new weakness, worked itself out in the predawn hours when I tended to wake long before Laird rose and started breakfast. I'd lie alone in my bed in the dark and sense the presence, just to the right in my mind's eye, of a patient listener behind a screen. The screen seemed made of translucent cloth, and the slight glow behind it vaguely outlined the profile of a head and shoulders. I never asked myself who it was, from the gallery of possible hearers; and I kept my eyes from ever looking toward the shape head-on. It—he, she or whatever—never spoke a sound but only heard me out as I worked at discovering my minimal needs and feasible hopes. I never asked it, point-blank, for answers—not yet anyhow. Its reliable presence seemed only to say that I had somehow to build my life on radical uncertainty, knowing only that I was heard by something more than the loyal but powerless humans near me.

Those curious sessions faded off, then stopped by the end of radiation. I've tried but have never had them again. No head and shoulders will pause to listen now; but it listened then, as the straits shrank down for my narrowest passage. And though the sensed presence never once spoke to my searchings, I'd settled at times in my previous life for slimmer consolations than that.

So even now I remain puzzled by those occasional friends and counselors who repeated one of the dumber TV-remedies of the time and urged me to let my *anger* out, to bellow my *rage*. Rage at whom or what, I couldn't guess. At a mindless cell proliferating in response to its haywire nature? At destiny and the whole design of my life, if it had a design? True, I felt a certain realistic dread of excess contact with medical doctors, but even my coldest freeze-dried doctor was hardly a fit object of rage—inhumanity is appallingly common in the upper reaches of that profession.

Best of all, with the help of friends, I managed to laugh a few times most days. Sometimes the rusty sound of my out-of-practice chuckle reminded me of how a gift as big as the tendency to laugh in the face of disaster is a literally biochemical endowment—my parents were still laughing naturally through me, as my brother often laughed beside me. And now I can realize that I was not just stunned in those months but was starting at last to concentrate my remaining strength on mere survival.

I was lucky that no one so much as mentioned a groundless but prevalent theory I learned of later—that cancer is a self-induced killer, willed on the victim by his own hateful or self-repelled psyche. On the contrary, the most interesting and eventually useful theory that I heard in my treatment came from a woman, a doctor from India, who—with a woman resident from Canada—was far the most humane person I met in radiation oncology. When the Indian doctor heard me say that I'd been subject to unexplained convulsions in infancy and that I'd had childhood problems in the coordination of arms and legs, she told me that spinal tumors were often congenital—present in the embryo and brought to life with us. If that was the case with me, then my body and mind had proved unusually resourceful for fifty years in sharing the tumor's ongoing life and evading its pressure. And couldn't that same mind and body turn now strongly against a guest who'd become a kind of lethal twin and force him out?

The only other staff radiologist with whom I spoke, a man from Texas, assured me that in my case they were "burning that sucker *out* of there." He beamed as if we were smoking a badger out of its den with certain success. My presiding oncologist saw me as seldom as he could manage. He plainly turned aside when I attempted casual conversation in the halls; and he seemed to know literally no word or look of mild encouragement or comradeship in the face of what, as I later learned, he thought was hurried death.

Did he think I was brewing my grievance against him, some costly revenge in the crowded market of malpractice suits? Did he shy from involvement with one more face that was hungry for life though already stamped *Dead*? My best guess from here is, he didn't know how to act otherwise; and he hadn't tried to learn. It's often said by way of excuse that doctors are insufficiently trained for humane relations. For complex long-range interaction with damaged creatures, they may well need a kind of training they never receive; but what I wanted and needed badly, from that man then, was the frank exchange of decent concern. When did such a basic transaction between two mammals require postgraduate instruction beyond our mother's breast?

As for possible tumor causes or triggers, when I

learned from scattered reading that mental depression can gravely weaken the immune system, I wondered if my maybe lifelong tumor hadn't started winning the upper hand in 1979. Late that April, while I was on campus for a brief mail-run, three men broke into my home in an especially brutal manner and tripped in me a summer-long bout of deep melancholia. The break-in, which was my fourth in six years, featured live gunfire between the burglars and a deputy sheriff (I innocently drove up minutes after the initial violence, when one of the men was still cornered in my house).

It would surely have involved me if I'd got home ten minutes earlier that afternoon, and the near-miss left me with the sense that my main place was now irreparably breached and was no longer feasible for life and work. Yet I couldn't decide to sell-up and move; many of my friends in town had similar problems. So I stayed on in my threatened place, and only months later when a friend actively intervened to lure me out of a pattern of agonized ceiling-gazing did I start to break the downward spiral of self-absorbed depression.

If I could keep my mind even-keeled now though—in the summer of '84—couldn't my immune system strengthen, with all the brands of help it was getting, and fight the lifelong tumor down? If the morning at Kinnereth had foundations in a real but inexplicable event, didn't it mean that my healing was assured but would come at me now through human agents? I never once thought that an instant would come when the tumor vanished and I'd stand upright and walk away with no further trial.

Since I'd been offered no guidance whatever from my hard-science doctors, nurses or therapists on the possibility or the techniques of mental imaging, I began to spend long stretches in practicing my own kinds of visual meditation. My initial methods were suggested in tapes sent to me by a physician friend in Mississippi. She herself had been ambushed years before by breast cancer, had refused a mastectomy but received radiation with serious burns and was very much alive still, working and interested in new cancer therapies. The tapes she sent me—in a box with tapes of the Bach flute sonatas—contained informal talks by Dr. Carl Simonton, an American pioneer in the field of visualization as a means of harnessing the body's powers of self-healing.

At the simplest level, Simonton suggested that an individual cancer-host should visualize in some personally vivid and appropriate way his or her tumor, then visualize his immune cells in the act of feeding on and destroying the tumor. Those visualizations should be practiced daily in whatever degree of calm a mind can muster for the effort, and the chance that those sessions could rouse and strengthen one's immune cells to attack an invader or an unwanted twin seemed at least worth a try. On that simple base then, I spent many hours that summer and fall in the solitary effort to think of nothing but how to mobilize my immune cells, which had somehow tolerated a dangerous guest, to join in the havoc wreaked by radiation on the literally irreplaceable cable between my brain and the rest of my body.

I even drew, with close attention to fantastic detail, a grotesque colored picture of the eel itself; and in long quiet stretches I'd study the drawing. Then I'd watch on the blood-colored screen behind my eyes as white blood cells surrounded the ravenous twin inside me and consumed its body. Not that I had great faith in the method. At times I felt that my brain was running some rejected sequence from Disney's *Fantasia*, the war of the good mice against the bad.

At such times I'd come close to sharing the general medical suspicion that alternate therapies amount to pointless shadowboxing. But surely the practice had to be harmless, no one looked on and laughed at my thoughts, the thoughts took up time which hung on my hands; and in a hard but invisible illness, slack time can be as devastating an enemy as disease itself. All these years later I'd still commend such visualizations to anyone besieged by renegade cells—whether cancer, resistant tuberculosis, another microbial disease, autoimmune diseases like rheumatoid arthritis and M.S., or even AIDS. I wouldn't suggest that the method "works" infallibly or often; but I suspect it did me some real good, if not in destroying tumor cells then in its gift of meditative calm, the sense it gave me of an ongoing grip on my mind at least.

If I try to recall the good moments that relieved those five weeks of radiation—the moments that I'm still sure were curative—I come up with a slim but powerful number of minutes or hours. All involve the carefully measured kindness of kin and friends. Among them a few spring to mind as especially useful. I've mentioned the attentions of Diana Betz, my physical therapist, to a body that was daily growing weaker and less magnetic. I'd lie on the floor three times a week while she patiently led me through all I could do—shaky arm and leg lifts, hip and torso swings.

In a silent honesty that our eyes shared, she and I knew that the efforts were producing no visible return of function or strength. From surgery on I could no longer raise my head or shoulders from a flat position on the living-room rug; too many nerves and muscles in my upper back had been dissected; too much scar tissue cluttered their paths. The illusory strength conveyed by the steroid had played itself out, and uncontrollable spastic jerks were beginning to twitch my weaker leg. Despite those omens Diana and I laughed a good deal (she took me out for my first lame meal, on a walking cane, to a fast-food diner—I'd missed an occasional bout of that bland baby food).

And with all Diana's professional goodwill and the trust she gave me in confiding problems of her own, our sessions kept me at least from loathing the flesh of a body which I'd always enjoyed (as had certain others) but which now was sliding past my control at a scary speed. And when Diana told me quietly at the end of a session that the previous night she'd dreamt of me walking unaided through the woods just outside the room where we worked, I responded with a promise that she and I together would walk in the beech woods by Thanksgiving.

It was a promise I couldn't keep, not literally; but I think I offered an acceptable substitute when Thanksgiving came—I returned to work. And the fact that a highly trained woman had dared to confess to that much concern for my ongoing life was a real contribution to my self-respect, a faculty that every disease aims at and pummels hard. Given my experience till then, any such confession from a medical male might well by then have proved perilously shocking; but from her resources of lifelong care, Diana made the stated hope of her dream seem humanly feasible, if not prophetic.

Then there was a daily stack of letters from friends and strangers. Some were too moving to read at the time, including the two that bade me solemn farewell at death's door and inspired eventual laughter. However welcome most letters were, I couldn't find words or even the impulse to answer any of them; and at times I came to dread the emotional bath they offered so intensely that I sometimes filed, unopened in a drawer, letters that seemed likely to trigger strong feeling—longing for that particular friend, say, or bitter nostalgia for our better days. And when I discovered some of the postponed letters by chance, six years later, they still had power to shake me.

If I'd been able to answer the letters, what could I have said to any friend but *Thanks, I'm here this instant anyhow*? Still, on balance, mail meant a great deal. My continued presence was wanted apparently by more than myself and the household company. And some of the best mail came oddly from strangers. I recall a short note from a strange woman who said that she had "a whole convent of nuns" praying for me and that "they get *results!*" Such homely assurance in the midst of a trial can sound like a far-off but usable message, helpful for anywhere from seconds to weeks. And since most American craftsmen in a particular guild eventually come to know one another, I hope it's clear that I don't intend a pointless display of distinguished friends when I say that—far from demonstrating the rivalry and backbiting of which we're often accused—fellow writers helped me especially with phone calls and letters.

A stranger to Philip Roth, for instance, approached him in Central Park that July of '84, said "Reynolds Price has spinal cancer"; and Philip was on the phone to me at once. It was a further Rothean pleasure for me that, when I tried to phone him back a few days later at a number he left on my answering machine, I got someone else's machine in Connecticut with a maniacally cheerful voice saying "Hi, this is Mr. Shower Door! Leave your number and I'll be right over!"—a mystery never solved;

Philip swore it wasn't him. John Updike learned of the situation from a magazine in his doctor's office and wrote me posthaste. Roth, Updike and I were born within a few months of each other—the class of 1932–33. We met early in our careers; and I'd noted with some amusement in 1968 that, consciously or not, Updike named one of the more predatory women in his novel *Couples* Constance Price Fox Roth.

Likewise encouraging and generous with visits and mail were Doris Betts and Frederick Busch. My great teacher Lord David Cecil wrote in the midst of a desolating loss of his own. Fred Chappell published a moving essay about our literary boyhoods together—I'd published his first stories and poems in the Duke literary magazine when I was a senior and he a freshman. Elizabeth Cox helped in dozens of practical ways. Horton Foote, Francine du Plessix Gray, Josephine Humphreys, Carolyn Kizer and Romulus Linney phoned, wrote and visited. Thomas McGuane sent letters and books. Howard Moss, on the verge of his own death, wrote and phoned often with his welcome voice like a wise and courtly marsupial's. Charlie Smith, about to publish his first novel, visited and offered to stay. Dave Smith and Lee Smith kept me well stocked with care and laughter.

Stephen Spender—past seventy-five and lame with bad knees—visited often, dedicated his *Collected Poems* to me and, not the least favor, gave me my first Sony Walkman. William Styron visited steadily, even in his own descending depression. Anne Tyler, whom I'd known since she entered my first freshman English class at the age of sixteen, offered to come and keep house and flew down to restate her offer in earnest. Eudora Welty visited and was in constant touch with funny clippings from country newspapers, phone calls in her shy still voice—

shy but reliable as any iron beam—and in letters of a radiance that meant as much as any I'd got in my life. Toni Morrison sent books and wrote with reminders of our bemused work together in the seventies for the National Endowment for the Arts.

And on the evening of July 11th of that first slow summer, as I lay on the floor exercising my legs, there came a call from a friend of more than two decades. She said simply "Reynolds, let me read you something." Then in a speaking voice nearly as rich as her song, Leontyne Price read me a poem which I'd written and given her in the 1970s. The poem is called "The Dream of a House," and in it I transcribed closely a recent dream of my own. My dreams are generally as boringly incoherent as anyone's; but this one was a shapely story that seemed worth recording, and I wrote it down fast.

It began with my being given a handsomely furnished house by a nameless man. After the man had guided me through rooms furnished with all the objects I'd ever wanted, he paused at a normal hall-closet and told me that behind the shut door was my final want, a life's companion. When I opened the door, there hung an actual crucified man in permanent agony—

> . . . *a man is*
> *Nailed to a T-shaped rig—*
> *Full-grown, his face eyelevel with mine,*
> *Eyes clamped. He has borne on a body*
> *No stronger than mine every*
> *Offense a sane man would dread—*
> *Flailed, pierced, gouged, crushed—*
> *But he has the still bearable sweet*
> *Salt smell of blood from my own finger,*
> *Not yet brown, though his long*
> *Hair is stiff with clots, flesh blue.*

The guide has never released my arm.
Now he takes it to the face. I don't resist.
The right eyelid is cool and moist.
I draw back slowly and turn to the guide.
Smile more dazzling than the day outside,
He says "Yours. Always."

I nod my thanks, accept the key.
From my lips, enormous, a blossom spreads
At last—white, smell strong as
New iron chain: gorgeous,
Lasting, fills the house. *

At the end of her reading, not mentioning the fact that the poem had clearly foreseen my state some eight years early, Leontyne only said "It means this now—you'll be all right." And she kept in close touch through the whole long tunnel.

To my knowledge that was the first arrival, from outside my immediate circle, of a message which came seven more times in the months ahead—the explicit and confident-sounding news that I wouldn't die, not of this ordeal. The message came mainly from women, though a few men joined them; and they each wrote or called with no prior collusion—most of them still don't know each other. One of the strongest and most ironic assurances came from a woman I hadn't seen for years, who'd herself been placed in an isolation chamber for several days shortly before while a capsule of radium was implanted in her body to bombard a pelvic cancer. She phoned me on a dismally low Sunday morning and, with no preface,

---

* "The Dream of a House" appears on page 195.

calmly said "I've called to tell you you're are not going to die of this cancer." Then she quoted the famous talisman lines from Psalm 91 that so many soldiers have taken to war,

> He shall give his angels charge over thee;
> To keep thee in all thy ways.

Soon she was dead but her word on me is still in force.

At moments of exhaustion those unsought assurances could ring a little crazily. I well understood that the vast majority of human prayers get No for an answer, if any answer at all. I knew that my threatened life was surely not an exception to that dark rule, despite my morning experience in Kinnereth. But as things sped downward in my mind and body that summer and fall, and a blank wall was all the end I could see, those promises from friends of unquestioned sanity carried more weight with my battered mind than most other messages. Bad as I often felt, they seemed oddly credible. And I'm still not convinced that I chose to trust them only because I needed to. Even now as I recall each one and the moment of its arrival, I can hear its battlefield-bulletin prose as welcome and trusty; and I take great care not to make empty promises to troubled friends unless, as I very rarely do, I have a firm sense of their ongoing luck.

Fear flooded in more than once toward the end of radiation as the weakness mounted and, in the last week of radiation, when an eight-inch-long second-degree burn developed on my neck and upper back. It was a suppurating lesion that required me to sleep on a sheepskin for weeks—the dry fleece cushioned the long wound while the steroid, which was meant to reduce inflammation, badly slowed repair throughout my body. If that was the state of my outer skin near the radiation site, imagine the state of my spinal cord an inch below at the focus of the fire. And tiny nipples of new flesh spread across my shoulders and the backs of my arms for months to come, then as mysteriously disappeared—another grisly gift from radiation.

I took my twenty-fifth and last treatment on August 8th. Laird Ellis left a week later to join his family. By then my walking was not just unreliable; I'd reached the new point where, several times a day, I'd be standing up with apparent strength; then suddenly with no warning or shove, I'd fall flat on my face to the floor. *Why?* No one volunteered a sure answer and I didn't press. But I hung on hard to the frozen oncologist's proposition— these were transitory results of swelling as the X ray fried its unblocked way to the core of the tumor, its old and most persistent growth. Only time or death could confirm or deny him.

Three weeks after the end of treatment, I went to what proved my final meeting with the man for two years. When he'd ordered me weighed and my blood checked for damage, he listened to the most hopeful summary I could manage of my recent symptoms (why could I never tell my doctors the depth of my fear?). Then he told me the baldly obvious. He'd given me all the spinal radiation I could receive in a lifetime, and he was now discouraged by my continuing loss of strength and motor power. The radiation had apparently failed to slow the tumor, much less stop it. He had nothing more to offer by way of human exchange than the patent fact that I'd have to wait now and see what resulted. Though he didn't define his implications, I understood them to be rapid death or slower total paralysis as the tumor

66

crushed out, one by one, the final crucial nerve connections between my lower body and my brain. He wanted me back in six weeks' time for another look; then he'd gauge my status.

I heard that, with harsh precision, as the arrangement of one more opportunity for a research scientist to update his files on one more failed experiment. When I asked him for practical suggestions of things to do in the interim (I was thinking of exercise, diet or medication— the last things many American physicians ever speak about), he gave me his blankest look, shrugged and said "Write the Great American Novel."

The best friend of my childhood, my cousin Marcia Drake Bennett, had brought me to the clinic that day and was standing beside me. The wife of a tirelessly humane family physician, she stared the oncologist dead in his eye and said "He's already written that."

Unsure as I was of her accuracy, I tasted triumph for one hot instant; and we both walked out, me dragging my right leg, leaning on the stout four-footed cane and both of us laughing as we reached the door.

For the next two weeks after Laird left, my friend Will Singer came out at the ends of his workdays in a cabinet shop. He cooked supper for me and stayed through the nights with such an uncomplicated calm of old friendship that I was able to write one more substantial poem about his stay.* Throughout those weeks I was still on high doses of the steroid, dexamethasone; and though it now gave little help to my walking, both Friedman and the oncologist recommended I continue it in hopes of reducing spinal inflammation. I took their advice and the

---

* "Hawk Hill" appears on page 205.

drug's notorious external signs soon began to appear, the mutilations of Cushing's syndrome. They included a swollen and sodden moon-face, the start of a buffalo hump of fat on the upper back, a roaring appetite for food and—worst—exhausting and unpredictable swings of mood.

With unstoppable manic force, the drug yo-yoed my mind from moments of unearned elation to black depression through most of my nights. Daytimes, with Will Singer off to work, I still sat idle in the living room or on the back porch watching the woods. I was still unable to write a word, read more than short stretches of a magazine or to do much more than think of what the near future concealed and to feel the chill numbness creep up both my legs past the knees. I was too low-spirited to know I was desperate, but in fact I was crossing a trackless desert. On one of those mornings, after I'd fallen to the floor several times and pain was rising, I called my brother Bill at his office in Raleigh. It was one of the few times I'd leaned hard on him.

He detected at once that I was in bad shape and drove straight to me. When he'd heard my fears that an irresistible landslide had started, he went downstairs and phoned Allan Friedman. I knew not to listen; and when Bill returned he told me only that Friedman had said there was nothing more that he could do now but go back in and remove more bone from my vertebrae, a minor decompression in hopes of some ease.

I heard that as the sound of surrender from the main doctor I'd trusted till now. If the situation had narrowed this drastically, should I quit too and join in the panic to clear out of life and neaten the landscape for all those near me? Given my tendency to oblige, the strange fact is not that I thought of conspiring with the cancer but that—for the first time, and with the fact of my morning in Kinnereth still clear but baffling before me—my mind made a crucial choice to resist. I'd refuse to join in quitting the field. The field was me. Where else could I go but off the roof or into a warm tub with one sharp razor blade—dead-heavy meat for my friends or kin to find and dispose of?

My first resolution was to deal with the pain. Far as it was from the pitch it would soar to eventually, back and shoulder pain was now a constant presence in the midst of my life. So shortly after Bill's call to Friedman, Bill and I went to the Duke Hospital brace shop where I spent an hour being measured by a man who might have arrived an instant before from a Dickens novel—so blindly absorbed in his curious work that he muttered and grinned as he sized my body. And when he emerged at last with the brace, it proved an equally Victorian artifact. Made of thick white canvas braced with stays and fitted with numerous chromium buckles, straps and laces, it covered my body from groin to armpit. In the wake of more than two decades of NASA's development of strong new fabrics and resilient plastics, I was being fitted with a brace my great-grandfather might have worn.

At the moment I didn't know three things—that I wouldn't be able to man it myself (I'd need a helper to deal with the laces and buckles in back), its bristling bulk wouldn't fit under any shirt I owned; and in the few months I tried to wear it, it would give me no perceptible relief. But I (and Blue Cross) bought it on the spot—the first of my many absurd investments in paraphernalia, commended by otherwise sane therapists, which proved either physically unusable or helpless or harmful.

*

Dazed as I was in the powerlessness, I saw one glaring and maybe impossible need to fill. Whatever my future in weeks or years, for a while at least I'd go on needing constant help for cooking, for tending the needs of a three-tiered house with numerous stairs, for driving and all the other chores that were speeding out of my present reach. From the vision of healing I'd had in July, from the love of friends and from my own animal will to endure, I had my reasons for refusing just yet to grant that this decline was irreversible. And no doctor had specifically warned me otherwise, not that I knew of.

So the hardest challenge I knew I faced was the prospect of hiring a practical nurse or some other tame and bearable companion. As a single man though, who'd lived mostly alone since the age of nineteen and whose close kin consisted of a brother with his wife and two daughters in a small house twenty-five miles away, I could see no natural place to turn. Charlie Smith had offered to bring his novel-in-progress down from Asheville and stay awhile. But anxious as I was, Charlie smoked like Pittsburgh; and I'd long since lost my will to live with smoke. The few other possible friends seemed wrong too—for reasons of mine always, not theirs. So the longest-postponed implication of a solitary life was now another blank wall at my face—*Live alone and you'll die alone*. For numerous days, dry-eyed as a snake, I weighed that cold fact in my mind. It felt as heavy as a stockyard axe.

3

I TURNED AGAIN to my cousin Marcia, the tall
and beautiful daughter of my mother's favorite nephew.
We were only a few months apart in age. And throughout our Depression-gypsy childhoods, because of our
parents' mutual fondness, Marcia and I often wound up
in the same town and school. Right through our undergraduate years together at Duke, we were each other's
main certainty of unquestioning trust and acceptance;
and all through our youth, we'd been constantly in trouble together for mischievous ventures and our shared
sense of the foolishness of things, even when we faced
the dead-earnest monetary and emotional crises of our
parents.

For twenty-odd years now Marcia had lived in
Goldsboro, an hour east of Raleigh, with her husband Paul
Bennett, the doctor who'd given Bill my eighteen-month
prognosis. We'd seldom met in recent years, though we'd
make contact on our birthdays and at Christmas. I knew
that their son and daughter were grown, living elsewhere;
and Marcia and Paul were not only generous to a fault but
were starting to rattle as a couple again in an outsized
house. Still it took me a few days to swallow my pride and a
lifelong dread of imposition.

But the moment I phoned to ask if they could tide me over till I was stronger, their answer was "Absolutely. Say when." They even managed to make me feel useful. Paul would soon be leaving for a month's work at a medical mission in Bangladesh, and Marcia was far from antici- pating life alone in a large house in a military town. So on August 27th she came to Durham, spent two weeks with me; then on September 13th she drove us to Golds- boro—me stretched on the back seat, queasy from my first real trip in months.

Once there, with Paul in Asia, Marcia insisted that I stay in her and Paul's huge bright room with its adjoining bath. She'd sleep ten yards away on the living-room sofa in case I fell in the night. I'd begun doing that too often now, especially in the bathroom on bone-breaking tile. But just the act of leaving my own house, fogged-in with worry as it was, made an instant improvement in my mind, however brief. And though I was still at the whim of a steroid that slammed my mind around like a crazed sparrow, I quickly started a different life.

Marcia and I would rise early, watch the televised news and eat a real breakfast (my steroid hunger raged on, and I'd begun at last to gain weight, which I tried to take as a sign that the radiation had done its work and was slowing its destruction). By now I was still just able to stand in the shower and to shave and dress myself, after which Marcia would leave on her errands. I'd settle in a chair in the bright bedroom and start to draw with Japanese brushes and colored inks in large sketchbooks.

I'd mix the drawing with short spells of reading. I'd started gingerly to read again—history and biography (the first book I recall was a new life of my distant cousin, the writer James Agee, who died at forty-five).

72

That would take me to lunchtime. Lunch consisted of a sandwich followed by butterscotch pudding, a boyhood favorite I'd barely eaten since. Then a genuine nap. Then Marcia and I would read to one another alternate chapters from various translations of the four gospels, the Acts of the Apostles and the letters of Paul. We'd pause to reflect on our quite different but civil views of our reading—her straightforward literalism, my more tortured dodgings. Without alluding to our motive, we plainly knew we were in a hard wind and were scratching for bedrock in the oldest place we'd been taught to look.

Late in the afternoon I'd turn back to drawing. Then I'd spend at least a half-hour session alone in which, after staring at my picture of the eel, I'd work at imagining my white blood cells in battle again, down its whole length. Then supper, the televised news again and maybe a lightweight video movie. A recent popular book, that several friends had sent me, recommended confronting disease with quantities of laughter. It's a prescription that's much more easily given than taken—try laughing on cue in the midst of depression—but I recall that Marcia and I had a several-night Dudley Moore comedy festival, then a run of forties classics—during all of which we managed to laugh, even occasional fits of the childish giggles that got us in hot water decades past; now we were also subject to snoring. Then early to bed.

It was a normal-sounding vacation routine, except that this was no one's vacation and that one of us was under assault while the other (Marcia, who was living with the knowledge of a darker prognosis than I even guessed) could only help with meticulous attention to small needs and the important chores of food, laundry and love. Though she and I talked the official radiation line—my spine was still inflamed from the work of tumor destruction; any day now, that would start to improve—I'm sure that we both understood we were ear-deep in mystery. Was I headed in fact for no cure at all or for something as unlikely as full restoration? Despite the uncertainties, for me those days and nights with Marcia were surely the best rescue available on Earth at the time.

With no conscious plan, the inkbrush drawings quickly grew in importance for me. Drawing had been the main work of my childhood, from the age of three or four. Well before I entered school, I'd begun it with my father in long sessions of drawing elephants. And from the age of five or six, with the rapt intent of a still-only child, I was making the normal child's paper copies of a visible world that I pursued with an avid hunger for what I thought would be big returns in power and pleasure.

I honestly think that, like all drawing children, I unconsciously shared the aim of the cave art of Cro-Magnon man. If I could truly make a world as nearly like the visible world as human hands and paints could manage, then the world beyond me would do my will or would at least let me pass as I went my way on private missions of hunger and daring. I had little sense of duty to show what was beautiful or comely; I was in the service of pure fidelity to what my eyes saw—the look of the world, the visible skin of nature and things as they strike the normal retina. And I'd kept the aim alive into high school before I slowly realized that I'd never make a first-rate painter. I was too much the slave of surfaces; my competent realism lacked the shine of an indwelling light that I sensed but couldn't show. All the same, through the years I'd continued to draw occasional portraits of friends and of bodies I hoped to know.

Now at Marcia's, within a few days—at a starting signal from outside—I recovered that feverish boyhood aim and a charge of that old energy. I'd told no more than two or three people of my morning experience in Kinnereth. For obvious reasons it still felt vulnerable and intensely private, but I soon told Marcia. And at once she asked me to illustrate the moment. I've never been good at working without some model before me, but to please Marcia I sketched a rough likeness of the crucial action—Jesus cupping the water to my head. As the lines moved down in ink on the paper, I knew I was suddenly concentrating for more than ten seconds on something better than the pain that roared all down my spine.

When I was done, rough as I'd drawn it, the sketch showed at least the relative positions of Jesus and me and the purple oblong that boxed my wound. The fact of regaining just that much on paper triggered the subject of all the dozens of drawings I'd make in the next two years. They were all, every one, meditations on the face of Jesus; and looking back through them now, I can wonder how I narrowed so much of my limited strength and hope for survival down to the space of a sheet of paper with a few brushed lines in search of the face that had driven Western art for more than a thousand years.

In my sketchbooks there are ferocious Christs like wilderness prophets with baleful eyes. There are big-eyed Byzantine Rulers of All. There are unbearded young Christs barely sighting their fate, compassionate healers, numinous shamans, elder brothers and implacable judges. And what I was doing in so much time and with such intense effort, I'm still by no means sure I can fathom.

I do know, however, that I was acting on one of my oldest curiosities—what was Jesus' actual appearance as he taught and healed in Galilee for a few short months before his death in Jerusalem in about the year 30?—and I know that the drawings became my main new means of prayer when my earlier means were near exhaustion. By now I'd asked a thousand times for healing, for ease and a longer life. But calamity proceeded, and even the repetition of "Your will be done" had come to sound empty. So the drawings were a sudden better way, an outcry and an offering. If they asked for anything, I suppose it was what I still ask for daily—for life as long as I have work to do, and work as long as I have life.

In retrospect I can wonder at the fact that, despite the hours spent working toward the face of Jesus, I seldom had the slightest thought that my ordeal might be a just punishment for past crimes and waste. I understood that through the years I'd caused real harm to more than one life, harm sufficient to bring down rage from a sane impeccable human judge. And even in the worst of my old desert treks, I'd taken more than one of the offered chances to repair the ruins I'd made in blind greed on some love or friendship.

I know that Jesus in the gospels speaks apparent contradictions on the subject of whether or not we're punished on Earth for our wrongs. So have many teachers in other traditions; but I've never been able to summon for long any lasting sense that the maker of the Pleiades, the force that powers black holes and quasars—the unimaginable violence of space—is keeping score on human deeds except maybe murder, the ruin of nature and systematic cruelty to the innocent and weak. I suspect we're the keepers of our own moral books; our only sure punishment comes from ourselves. So the faces my hand laid down on paper in those long days, imposing as some of them still are in their piercing gaze, only underlined what I've always heard as the core of Jesus' meaning as it burns through the surface of his surviving words—to me it seems to be *All is forgiven where forgiveness is sought: all but the failure to trust that forgiveness.*

Partly too in the drawings, I think—since I'd proved unable in recent days to write more poems but was aching to start—my unconscious mind was inventing its slow way toward its best work. To reach that end, it moved me back through five decades to the simple beginnings of my adult trade as a narrative writer. Once it had me there, it forced me to learn again, by hand, the pleasure of making orderly pictures that copied the visible world and likewise altered it through the eyes of inward hope and dread. Once finished, the pictures offered those findings to the only people near me. At the end of each day, I'd show the day's drawings to Marcia and Paul, once Paul returned from his mission in Asia. They saw them as the natural, workmanly though hardly dazzling, products of honest and harmless labor. They never offered to run to a framer; they never asked to have a drawing, but their interest was steady. And I'd draw more the following day, always with music in my ears from the Sony Walkman that I was quickly wearing out.

But with all the health that flowed from the drawings and music, a poisonous weight of idle time still banked up around me. In any waking day I'd be at loose ends at least half the time; and then I'd founder in the rising pain, the numbness that crept on higher up my thighs and hips, then past my waist. And I could only stare at the block in my path—the future I'd get. A silent mark of my deepening descent into bouts of mental blindness (I was still on the steroid) is visible in the fact that even my daily calendar ceases once I reached Goldsboro. *Benchmarks are meaningless; I won't last to read them.*

An even more visible mark stared at me one morning as I staggered into Marcia and Paul's big bathroom and glimpsed my naked waist in the mirror. Overnight my gut had collapsed. My waist was suddenly ten inches bigger than it'd been the previous night. In those few hours, with no prior weakness, I'd lost all power to contract the abdominal muscles that ringed and contained my guts; and I've never got it back. None of my trousers would begin to reach round me. Marcia went out and brought me several jaunty track suits with huge elastic waists. I chose the dark blue with a red racing stripe and wore little else for weeks to come.

I'd been a fairly presentable man; this was my first big loss of ground in the department of personal pride, but I don't recall having the available energy to mourn for an instant. In a day or two, as my legs and feet swelled from inactivity, I could no longer wear any of my shoes. I'd gone that fast from a size nine to a wide size twelve.

In another few days I'd lost the strength to stand in the shower and was forced to sit on a stool and wash. My legs, that had managed the considerable distances between rooms in Marcia and Paul's house, could barely walk me in for meals now. And after Paul left, and Marcia and I set out one afternoon to get me a routine chest X ray for a nagging cough, I got myself halfway out the door; then my right foot suddenly refused to lift from the floor and step forward. It was the first such absolute refusal since I'd found I couldn't run, months back in the parking lot.

The difference was that then I couldn't jog along. Now the sole of my right foot was nailed to the floor. I couldn't budge it and had to wait on a chair while Marcia phoned for a strong male friend. When he finally reached us twenty minutes later, I clung round his neck while he carried me on his back to my bed. For a few more days, unpredictably, my legs would work for short jerky stretches if I leaned heavily on the cane. But the landslide was plainly an avalanche now.

Marcia still had the native optimism that had got her through a hard childhood, but even she admitted now that something awful was underway at frightening speed. I recall the sober look on her face as she stood by my bed that afternoon and said "We don't know what's going on here, do we? But we're riding it out. I'm with you straight through, for however long it takes." Neither one of us guessed aloud what the *it* might be that was bearing down now.

I've said that Marcia and I had stood beside each other through the childhood terrors of poverty and family disorder. She'd never been less than entirely loyal and openhearted in all our time since infancy, so I trusted her—we were in deep dark. As always the only way *out* was *through*. I'd not only reached a new low of weakness; my immobility was continuing to swell both legs grotesquely from the knees down; I was falling almost daily and could no longer raise myself. One morning we'd had to call a man who was mowing grass two doors down to lift me from the floor. The constant pain along my spine grew hotter by the day.

I'd developed a pressure sore on my tailbone; and the steroid was blocking its healing. That required careful treatment with an old hairdryer to form a protective scab, a slow process when you're sitting on your tailbone for most of the day. My cough proved to be a symptom of a partially collapsed lung, another triumph for the radiation. I'd been warned that the steroid might cause mood swings; but once a drug has gripped your mind, such warnings give no consolation—you simply forget them. And now my steroid-cooked range of feelings was growing more wildly erratic than ever. I'd be unrealistically cheerful one moment, with bursts of popular songs from my youth, or despairing the next.

In rare calm moments I was coming to see that the frozen oncologist's five-percent warning was enacting itself. Whatever harm the radiation might yet do the cancer, it had meanwhile irreparably scorched many crucial veins and nerves inside my cord. I was losing the use of both my legs, almost surely for good. I'd after all won my place in the top five percent of human beings who get four thousand rads of X ray to the spine.

It was in the first days of confronting that fact that I had a second—and last, till now—uncanny experience. This one was different in kind from the first. It came as a sound, one syllable, not an action; and it came late at night. I was still at Marcia's; and Paul was still gone, so she and I were alone in the house—she sleeping some yards away on the sofa. I'd waked in the dark and, against my better knowledge, was poring through my somber prospects.

A realistic estimate included paralysis, dependence on others, untouchable pain and the absence of work. Maybe I'd really been tricked in my "vision." Maybe death or worse was near; quadriplegia now seemed worse than death. Death would solve at least the other quandaries. In that black trough I remember looking up to the ceiling and addressing what I must have thought was God, the last unchangeable bafflement—"How much more do I take?"

A long silent pause, then a voice at normal speaking strength said the one word "More." Neither male, female nor repellently neuter but thoroughly real and near at hand, though well beyond sight and unheard by Marcia. *More* then. No ease yet. And no further reply of any such presence and unyielding foresight came thereafter in times at least as staggering, when all the answers I got came in other forms—mainly human help.

Next morning, not mentioning the word in the night, I asked Marcia to call her minister at the Methodist church and ask if he'd bring me the sacrament of communion. I'd been raised in the Methodist church myself; and while I'd stopped attending years back, I kept a strong respect for the primary sacrament—communion. I was sure it was a possible shaft onto whatever help might come. If I'd thought clearly I might have seen that Marcia and I could share the rite on our own with no need other than bread and wine and Jesus' words as he founded the custom on the night before his arrest and death. But she called her minister and he agreed.

He came to my bedroom on a clear hot morning; I sat in my chair, no one else near. He read the words from the Gospel of Mark—*This is my body, this is my blood, do this in memory of me*—then he fed me communion. Since my first taste in childhood of the meager portions of bread and wine—and long before I knew of the dogma wars that have raged round the act—I'd been a natural believer in the actual presence of Jesus in the swallowed fragments. Unlike Roman Catholics, I felt no need to sense the elements as literal human flesh and blood; but perhaps as intensely as any mystic, in the slow eating that one morning, I experienced again the almost overwhelming force which has always felt to me like God's presence. Whether the force would confirm my healing or go on devastating me, for the moment I barely cared. No prior taste in my old life had meant as much as this new chance at a washed and clarified view of my fate—and that from the hands of a strange young minister in a room which didn't belong to me. In many calmer hours to come, I'd know that my answer to the one word *More* was three words anyhow—*Bring it on*.

As the weeks in Goldsboro staggered ahead, sheltered as I was by my kin, I saw again the main practical problem. Where and how would I live from here on, for however many days or years? Any hope of living alone again in my own house was surely deluded. I could never ask Bill, his wife and two daughters—however caring—to uproot themselves and join me in Durham (their house could not have held all of us without severe crowding). Marcia and Paul had said, with plain honesty, that they'd volunteered for the whole duration of my needs. But good as it was to have that strong net waiting beneath me, I couldn't yet think of leaving my home, the site of my work—both writing and teaching—and the shelter of so much rewarding friendship and coupling. So that confusion knotted itself round all my other unanswered questions.

Then one big answer came, unthinkable in its generosity. I've mentioned traveling to Israel in the fall of '83 with a friend. He was Daniel Voll, who'd graduated from Duke in 1983 after auditing my seminar in narrative writing. His ambitions for writing were high, and he'd spent some months at my house that summer before heading off in February '84 on a fellowship to study for the better part of a year in South Africa. We'd corresponded through those months; I'd phoned him when I got first word of the cancer. But nothing had prepared me for the apparently effortless decision he'd make before leaving Cape Town. He gathered that I needed constant help. *Right*. He wrote me at once; then phoned me to say that, if I could use him, he'd come to Durham and give me that care till I was walking on my own again. He set no conditions whatever on the offer. No amount of time was specified, no wages were mentioned, and none were paid at any point—he wouldn't hear of it.

Recalling the two-year trough of grief and helplessness that I slogged through after tending my own father's quick death of cancer, I wondered if I mustn't tell Dan to take some more direct path into whatever life and work he'd have. By now though, I also knew I was a beggar with bone-slim choices. And I knew Dan well enough to know he'd given the matter long thought before making his offer. So I thanked him; left all arrangements to him—when he'd leave Africa, when he'd reach me—and I waited on with Marcia in Goldsboro, drawing and watching my disintegrating body.

Young as he was, Dan Voll had great stability of thought and feeling and a fearless drive to solve all soluble problems *now*, not an hour from now. His intelligence, his mature curiosity and attention to the world and his excellent wit were further assets. So when he reached Goldsboro in early October, I felt for the first time in weeks strong moments of hope that I might live to walk again and to see my cancer eradicated. We stayed on with Marcia for another few days till Dan recovered from an intercontinental cold. Then on October 8th we returned to Durham and began the effort to find ways back to a normal work life.

4

M<small>Y</small> HOME was a fairly conventional three-level house of the early 1960s—two bedrooms, two baths and a study upstairs, living room and kitchen on the ground-floor level, and a dining room and laundry room downstairs. Short of offering spiral staircases, the physical realties of the house could hardly have been worse for anyone in my present situation; but I was still a long way from facing that fact—*I'll soon be ready to navigate steps; for now I can pull myself to the bedroom by clutching a railing and hauling my body up with main force.* That clumsy skill worked for a few days as Dan went quickly to work, clearing whatever obstructions I'd concede to.

He added grab bars to the bathroom walls, so I could haul myself on and off the toilet; he installed a padded shower bench. He rented a wheelchair for outside ventures. I was still opposed to buying one; it seemed a premature surrender, and I used the rented chair very seldom. With my immediate needs provided for, Dan settled into the spare bedroom and set up his own office in the dining room, which was almost beyond my reach downstairs. Soon he'd begun work on two commissioned articles about his South African stay—one for *Vanity Fair*, one for *Harper's*. Soon, as well, he was cooking dinners for my close friends,

friends were coming to stay, there was warm encouraging company in the house for the first time in months. And though I wasn't yet writing fiction, my drawing went on almost fiercely.

In late October for the first time in six weeks, I wrote a few lines in my daybook. .

> Long silence here—six weeks of days
> When numbness climbed my body: this chimney
> With ample footholds, a shuddering fire.
> But now as dead leaves stroke the house
> And crazed squirrels race to hide (from themselves)
> The deluge of beech- and hickory-nuts,
> I warm again to the heat of life—
> A promised stretch of upright time,
> The vision of cure in Kinnereth;
> The calm white-hot assurance
> From six sane friends that I'll survive
> In human, useful, usable form
> Are credible again.
>   And these words boil up
> Sure, unhedged as a year-old boy's
> Blue gold-edged eyes.

(Friends had called by that morning with their young son.)

By October 21st I'd completed a gradual withdrawal from the steroid. I'd been in its grip for most of the time since early June. To the last milligram it flung and bloated and humiliated me, and for no more apparent good than a few days' strength at the start of radiation. Now my only drug was self-prescribed Tylenol for pain. In fact it amounted to a teaspoon of water on a major bonfire; but for any veteran of an American childhood like mine—with a mother ever-ready at the pillbox—it seemed a gesture in the faint direction of control anyhow. I'd also resumed regular physical therapy with Diana Betz.

She was plainly alarmed at my loss of strength in the weeks away. In Goldsboro I'd neglected the few exercises I could still do; but however badly I'd failed myself and Diana's hopes in me, she calmly took up where we'd left off and stayed right with me. At least her regular visits offered a small goal. Some of my weakness might well have resulted from steroidal wasting of muscle and bone, a common phenomenon. We might regain that much. Meanwhile with Diana's visits, and with Dan's invention of further techniques for getting me up and down stairs—I'd hang on for dear life to the stair railing; and Dan would lift my feet up the risers, one by one with sheer main strength (my knees would still lock for a few seconds each)—I no longer had quite as much self-pity to lean back into. If I couldn't begin to write again soon, it was strictly my fault or the Holy Ghost's.

Still, it was mid-fall and work didn't come. The first third of *Kate Vaiden* waited on my desk, untouched since May. Then chance, or something more conscious, intervened. In early November I got a call from Hendrix College in Arkansas, an excellent liberal-arts college where I'd given readings and seminars a few years back. The strong theater department at Hendrix was under the direction of Rosemary Henenberg. She'd previously directed my play *Early Dark* with student actors and with good results, and it was she who called now to ask if I'd accept a commission from the department to write a play for their students.

As I listened to her voice on the phone, I understood

clearly that this was the first piece of work I'd been offered since Marcia asked me to illustrate my vision, and I heard the summons as coming from some benign source more complex than a college. But first I made a full disclosure; I told Rosemary they'd be taking a bet on a man in trouble, with a clouded future.

She'd heard nothing of my situation, but her Texan voice was undeterred—would I write the play?

I was more than ready to say I'd try.

A few days later we signed an agreement, and I was able to start at once on an idea that came almost simultaneously with the commission. I'd write about a young man and woman whose experience were within the emotional grasp of student actors, yet my theme would be pertinent to all human ages—the difficulties of strict fidelity in love and friendship and toward our kin. In its concern with a hard day in the life of a couple married for one year and threatened with ruin, the play would be founded on things I'd heard about my parents' troubles well before I was born and of course on my own sins and losses.

My mother and father had five hard years together before conceiving a child. My arrival proved the occasion for a drastic renewal of their vows; and from early childhood, I'd tried to imagine what they'd endured from one another to reach the place where I was welcome. And though the scenes came slowly at first, as if they walked from a great distance toward me through some dense medium, it was soon clear that I'd stumbled on a useful choice in returning—here again, as I'd done in the drawings—to the headwaters of my own life.

For the next two months then, I sat in a chair in my bedroom and filled lined pages in a legal pad—one summer dawn a young wife gives her inattentive husband an ultimatum: stop drinking, stop running wild with your friends; and tend to your marriage, starting today. With the first week of work, however slow and against the grain of the past jangled months, I tasted the old lost pleasure of mimicry and vicarious life, the pleasure of becoming people other than me and with other dilemmas as grave as mine.

My physical health was still declining steeply. The numbness had climbed my back to the neck and my chest to the height of my nipples; my legs were weaker and constantly roared like renegade dynamos with violent electrical storms of sensation beneath the dull surface. The back pain only ground in deeper. There were times each day, for hours at a stretch, when my whole body felt caught in the threads of a giant hot screw and bolted inward to the point of screaming. At such times I'd lie on the bed, chew the corner of a dry pillowcase in dumb confusion, pray for relief or perfect my knowledge of every nick and crack in the ceiling.

But my mind was improving in at least one department. I'd finally cranked one badly stalled engine—or had it cranked by the play commission. I was writing for an hour or more each day, a page or two in the ongoing lives of my young characters. Slow as it went, I knew as well as any crossroads mechanic that starting a cold engine is half the battle; and I never let my writing faculty seize up again, not till now at least.

When the play, called *August Snow*, was finished late in the winter of '84, I was finally freed to move back into my abandoned study, switch on the computer and take *Kate Vaiden* up where I'd left her. She'd boarded the train to Norfolk, Virginia—the first runaway of her renegade life, her meeting the man who'd father the child she'd choose to abandon. And very soon after I resumed her wry and indomitable voice, I found myself deep again in one old pleasure—full immersion in an alternate life, in a substitute fate with all-new problems.

The fact that I'd never before attempted a long story in the voice of a woman only intensified the regular help I found in the writing. For however many hours a day, I was not only challenged to invent and tell a story; I was also licensed to become a person as different from me as any I'd watched in thirty years of making up people—a woman with a fate that was harder than mine but who finally rounded on her torment, her own collusion in forty years of loss, desertion and pain, and cut her way clear with a skittish courage and a feisty tongue I could hide in at least.

In mid-November I'd also begun again to make brief notes in my calendar. They record a few dinners out with friends, more friends coming to stay overnight and a trip with Dan to visit Marcia and Paul again, with me in better spirits. Mostly though the notes show that I stayed in the close confines of home—to the point eventually of a neurotic dread of leaving, a siege of near-agoraphobia that kept me indoors and most others out. I'd work all day and sometimes past midnight, with time out only for meals and rest and occasional drawings.

In the evenings Dan and I watched a long slew of video movies, a virtual survey of movie history; and we read good novels aloud to each other. I recall Fitzgerald's *Tender Is the Night* and Willa Cather's *My Mortal Enemy*. In that way I could go weeks at a time with no compulsion to leave the house and dilute the focus of my fixed gaze at the narrow circle I'd drawn around my few urgent needs—work and healing or learning to die if death was required. The major aim, I told myself, was silence and an even-keeled progress through time. And the first unusual action of the fall was when Dan cooked a turkey breast, yams and green beans and maneuvered me down in the loathsome rented wheelchair to the dining room for Thanksgiving dinner—my first meal there in months. The two of us ate at the heart-pine table that was now Dan's desk; then both returned to our writing jobs as if world peace depended on our diligence.

I learned years later that some of my acquaintances inferred from my seclusion that I suffered from AIDS, a threat which was only a few years old. Three of my close friends had died or were dying of the plague whose cause was only discovered in the year of my first surgery. The friends were Stuart White, who with prodigious understanding directed my first play in New York; Tom Victor, the uncannily watchful photographer of writers and dancers; and Jim Boatwright, one of my best colleagues, a splendid teacher and editor. Stuart sickened before I knew of my cancer; he died, I think, while I was in radiation. We'd talked on the phone for as long as I thought he knew me. Tom was failing rapidly in New York and then in his sister's house in Michigan; Jim went from health to a ghastly seventy-five pounds in his house in sun-battered Key West; and I'd speak with him on the phone at intervals, again as long as he knew my voice.

At the start of my trouble, only Stuart had died. The other two had yet to learn of their infection and were calling me to sympathize and laugh. Soon though it was they who were growing transparent and literally vanishing—their voices frailer with every call, each of them tragically shamed by their fate. Stuart and Tom were years younger than I; Jim was my age. I might well have shared their desolate fate to die on the forward edge of a disease as awful as any in its flat defiance of the literal core of human life, the body's joy in transmitting itself; but the fact was I didn't.

That assault missed me. Unknowingly, I'd somehow dodged that lunge. And the possibility that strangers might have thought I was in hiding, wasting with AIDS, never dawned on me till a writer from the *Washington Post* flew down in 1986 and informed me that his editor had instructed him, among other things, to investigate the rumor. By then at least I was able to assure him that I'd missed one more of my possible endings.

With all the fears of moving outside my own tight rooms, I also gave myself "practical" reasons for holding back from the outside world. My legs wouldn't get me out to the car, I still resisted the rented wheelchair, and I was months away from learning how to deal with the potential daily bladder and bowel embarrassments to which the crippled are especially subject. I was also still half convinced that I'd be walking soon. *Why lean on a crutch or on invalid wheels that raise as many problems as they solve?*

And why force oneself on a world that's literally bent on repelling your presence and movement? As any cripple knows, the vast majority of American streets, houses and commercial buildings still take the howlingly ludicrous view that no human being will ever live past the age of forty. In their architects' fantasy world, none of us will ever be slowed by age or illness, never be hobbled by arthritis or paralysis; and none of us, for whatever other thousand reasons, will someday be in serious need of the cooperation of bricks, concrete and the watchful sympathy of able-bodied others.

Before I'd ever known of the tumor, I'd arranged a normal sabbatical leave from Duke for the teaching year '84–85; so I had no compelling reasons to visit campus. Life in the confines of my house was now consumed in writing by day and, most nights, watching video movies—sometimes as many as five a week. Jeff and Lettie Anderson would join Dan and me on Saturday nights; and the four of us would crowd onto my brass bed and laugh through more of the Three Stooges' "Greatest Hits" or what other comedies we could bear.

Dan handled the shopping and all the chores connected with running a sizable house, all but cleaning the rooms and doing the laundry. My friend Dorothy Brame did those jobs every Wednesday with unfailing cheer (it was she who'd brought me the sheepskin pad for my oozing neck burn). The friends whom I really wanted to see were calling by loyally. Through that long fall and winter then, I continued under self-imposed house arrest. Dan and I even ate on portable tables in my bedroom.

As I've said, the house arrest was partly neurotic—*Home's the only place I'm safe*—but the self-enforced confinement served two excellent ends. It gave me, again, the silent time and space I needed to focus inward on my weakened self-composure and on the moment-by-moment task of healing, or of partly earning the healing I'd wangled in Lake Kinnereth. And the silence likewise left my remaining energy free for work and a few good simple friendships. Sex had mysteriously still made no strong demands for service, though the requisite hormones were still at work—my voice and beard were unaffected, I was still potent, and my genitals lost no more sensation after surgery.

Did the months of seclusion harm me at all; did they feed the tumor? If I turn through the new calendar that I kept from late December '84 onward, I can see in the meticulous entries that I rapidly developed an obsessive fascination with my body and its momentary symptoms. A day at a time I notched off the rises in numbness and weakness, the number of lengths I walked each day in the parallel bars Jeff had built for me just off the back porch. *Walk* was not the honest verb. By then I was dragging myself along with heavy arm pressure on the metal side-bars, unable to stand alone—my knee locks had finally quit for good.

I noted that an extra twenty-five pounds of body weight, a legacy of my steroid hunger, were compounding my physical torpor. I charted the increasingly powerful storms in the nerves of my back and legs. That was a state which worsened daily and resembled nothing so much as an immense amplification of the pins-and-needles sensation of a limb asleep. And unpredictable internal rages gave me the sense of a white-hot scalding down my spine to my feet.

I noted that Dr. Friedman phoned me every few weeks with clear concern and the hope to see me, a hope I resisted. I hadn't seen him since late August '84, my last visit to Duke Hospital. That day in separate interviews, both he and the frozen oncologist had made it plain that they'd done what they could for me—the tumor remained inoperable; I'd had all the radiation I could take, to the spine at least. So from there I'd grabbed the bit in my teeth; and I ran hard with it for the next ten months—the drawings, the play, *Kate Vaiden*, no daybook poems from fall to late winter, love and friendship and very little else were what I'd chosen as certainties. Whatever intangible fears I was fleeing, when it came to thinking of Duke Hospital, I knew precisely what I was fleeing—an actual building and a very few members of its staff who (in my mind, for right or wrong) now meant only pain and death.

*

February 7th '85 would have been my mother's eightieth birthday, an inconceivable age for someone as vital as
she when she died at sixty. On the day itself I wrote my
first daybook poem in nearly four months; and it came as
a prayer to her, my first caretaker.

> *Dear girl, dead twenty years*
> *But hot as new blood,*
> *You're eighty today.*
>
> *Do you see me here—*
> *Stove-up at fifty-two,*
> *Numb as a plate?*
>
> *Can you beg for help?*
> *Will your own starved lips*
> *Move once to save me?*

There was no uncanny reply to the question, no sense of
Mother or Father's awareness; but my memories of their
own endings were steady companions—strong open-eyed
surrenders.

By the early spring of '85 though, I was still obsessively
noting my increases of trouble. Typical of the roller-
coaster entries are days like these:

March 10 - A strong day—strongest since Christmas
at least, though very numb and "noisy" (neuro-stat-
ic in legs).
March 12 - The worst day yet—back and legs—but I
was strong for physical therapy with Diana at 4:30.
Then an extremely uncomfortable evening.
April 12 - A bad tumble at the bathroom door.
Sprained my knee. But afterwards a buoyant day of

good work, good physical therapy. Sore but bearable back.

April 22 - An appallingly bad day—legs, arms, back: all much worse. Called Paul Bennett, who'll phone back tomorrow with advice about new doctor to consult. Began part three of *Kate*—30 lines.

By late April then I knew I was either losing grip on my mind or was gaining slow strength, with normal setbacks, or was speeding to die. In the face of the alternate highs in which I'd literally sing at my desk or the lows in which I'd lie on my bed and howl "I'm dying and nothing can help me," Dan Voll somehow found the brave grace to insist that I was surely not dying—I was plainly alive and must scrounge out the new ways to fight new demons.

Dan would sometimes have to counter-howl to silence my terrors and break the near-alliance I was trying to make with death. Many days we'd shout our fears and promises back and forth between our rooms. And surely the fact that we'd each spent our childhoods with tolerant parents, free to say what moved or feared us, was a huge gift now—toward both my healing and Dan's deep patience that never broke for as much as a moment.

Eight years later Dan would quietly tell me that he felt those days had been his Vietnam—he was fourteen and safe in Illinois when Saigon fell. But here with me, whatever fears he may have felt alone in his room, he never for an instant betrayed disgust at my polar moods or gave me the satisfaction of glimpsing death reflected in his calm eyes. With any less help than his—and I still don't know where I'd have found his equal—I can't imagine I'd be alive now. Recompense for such a gift does not exist.

*

At Dan's steady urging then, I called Paul Bennett and asked him to find me a humane neurologist with whom I could break my phobia of returning to medical care with its dangerous answers to ultimate questions I refused to ask—*How much longer? What next?* Two days later on April 24th, Dan drove me the 120 miles to Greenville, North Carolina. As we went I shuffled through an abbreviated copy of my records at Duke (Friedman had sent it at my request). Almost at once my eye snagged on the radiation oncologist's summary at the end of my five weeks. In a very few words he said in effect that, in view of my continued loss of motor function throughout my treatment, he felt that the outlook was pessimistic. I stopped reading there.

At his office in Greenville, Dr. Ross Shuping spent an uninterrupted seventy minutes examining me and observing my walk as I hung my arms around his and Dan's shoulders and dragged myself across five yards of floor. Then he sat us down and confronted me eye-to-eye with clear and believable conclusions. They were the first I'd listened to, or been willing to hear, from an informed observer in more than eight months. He said I was obviously in bad shape for walking; that hard reality would likely not improve. I was, equally obviously, not dying fast (was he sure of the claim or merely bold enough to risk the gambit in hopes of rousing my will and my stunned immune system?).

He further said that I might well have many years to live; how was I going to navigate them? What I needed, he said—and he urged me to find it immediately—was a thorough course of re-education at a rigorous in-patient rehabilitation center that could show me one of two things: how to lead an independent life with my losses or, failing that, how to use whatever strengths I had and might go on having in whatever future I got with companions.

My response was elation. And the burst of excitement was barely daunted by the tour we took that same afternoon of the state rehab center there in Greenville—a big complex of therapy rooms, job-retraining rooms, gyms, training kitchens (how to cook from a wheelchair) and bed- and bathrooms in which paraplegics, even quadriplegics, were undergoing the harder-than-Marine-Corps basic training in how to haul, drag or stump one's way back into life with no favors asked. The kind nurse who showed us round the center estimated that my needs might require eight to ten weeks, unbroken, with them. No one else had remotely suggested such a clear course for me. Dan was initially as unfazed as I by the sight of truly hard-core rehabilitation, and he shared my excitement. On the way home we stopped in Goldsboro to tell the good news to Marcia and Paul. And that night at home, I wrote in my calendar,

A sense of hard problems but great hope.... After this first car-trip since 25 December, I was not exhausted. Bed at 10:20. Dan's help was beyond praise.

Years later I can't explain why I lost that momentum. For in fact I waited ten more weeks before entering the rehab program at Duke (Dan Voll suggests that I was probably intent on writing *Kate Vaiden*, which he calls "the essential rehab"). In that two-and-a-half-month pause, I'd investigated programs as far off as the one in Greenville, one in western North Carolina and the famous Rusk Center in New York City. I'd rejected them all as either too far from home and friends or, frankly, too desolatingly merciless in their demands for the heroism of unaided gimp-life. A tentative sign of improving mental health was my willingness from now on to call myself either gimped or crippled—not disadvantaged, specially challenged or beatified-by-pain (Chuck Close, the splendid and recently quadriplegic American painter, shares my commitment to the label *gimp* and has told me of a beautifully precise name he's found for the able-bodied who loom above us in rooms and on streets—he calls them *temporarily abled*). Once Dan had thoroughly checked out the good but less intense program at Duke however, I still held it off.

I worked on rapidly through the spring of '85 with *Kate Vaiden*; and though I continued compulsively noting high and low days in the calendar, my regular entries began to show a marked further opening to friends and movement. In May we visited Marcia and Paul again, this time at their beach house near Morehead City. It was a trip I couldn't have thought of taking only weeks before. And on June 28th I paid my first visit to Duke Hospital since the previous August. Bill Price and Dan went with me. We saw the neurologist who'd diagnosed my tumor, and he arranged for me to enter the rehab program in early July.

On July 7th, a day before admission, the calendar shows that my new hope wasn't fending off losses.

A week in which standing and walking (on cane or walker) were virtually impossible. First such sustained loss.

But on through the early days of rehab, still I fiercely denied that my losses were permanent. Whenever my assigned trainer—a pleasantly tough young physical therapist named Wilkie Thomas—would remark that I was paraplegic, I'd correct her: "I can walk. I just need help."

Yet my calendar shows that on the third day, Wilkie told me "Walking is now an unrealistic goal." She repeated it firmly the following day when I brought her to my room on the ward and demonstrated the few steps I could manage in a walker. When she nodded in silence, wheeled me back down to the gym and told me to rise in the parallel bars, I failed completely, falling back into my chair.

Later that afternoon however, I lay alone on a mat in the gym and performed fifty-two strong leg lifts, a lifetime record. For whatever reason, a last burst of current ran from my brain down through both legs for that final show; then never again. Just in those three days since leaving home, my legs had lost contact with my mind; and I've never stood since, not on my own steam. But I threw myself at what I could do with a hungry will I'd never known before in a gym, and the next month went by faster than I'd planned.

For me one of the liberations of the time was the general absence of doctors from our lives and the resulting sense that we were a marooned island of damaged men and women intent on bringing ourselves to a state of repair that would let us visit the mainland again. A few of us with recent injuries got doctor-attention in lightning visits, but in a four-week stay I saw my original diagnosing neurologist for a total of under half an hour. He always came to my room with a solemn train of students; and he talked much more at them than me, which I didn't mind—I was still half courting medical silence. I can't recall a single visit to any of us from a licensed physician in our main arenas of daily work—the gym, the kitchen, the johns, the distant pool. They left all hands-on human transactions to the better-equipped.

My surgeon Allan Friedman, who wasn't strictly speaking a member of the rehab staff, stopped by the room late one afternoon for fifteen minutes. It was our first face-to-face encounter in eleven months. He asked me to rise and show him my gait. I managed a few spastic steps in the walker, then sat on my bed. He asked me to rise on my own but I couldn't. Though I'd kept him informed about my losses, the times he phoned me, he was visibly shocked now at my heavy losses, said little more and left very soon, not to return through the rest of my stay.

I've wondered since but have never asked—did Friedman suddenly wish he'd gone back inside me the previous June and taken the high risk of hauling out the bulk of the tumor with what were then inadequate tools? In any case, I've never spent a conscious moment in wishing he'd tried more drastic measures in spring '84 or the ensuing year of racing uncertainties. What happened in and to me, happened, I more than half believe, for an interesting reason that—nine years later—has begun to be visible. I rest now in that.

In the rehab program itself, our needs were filled and our challenges set by professionals from the nursing and physical therapy staffs. Every one of them (I knew them all and saw no exception) was admirably skilled, devoted and unflagging in their hours with us. Most of the therapists were white women in their twenties or early thirties; I recall two men—one black, one white. Apparently the emotional demands of the job (and no doubt the pay) drive many into other fields after a few years. But while I worked with young Duke therapists in twice-a-day sessions, morning and afternoon, I saw they were all committed to sensible help at least with good-natured patience; and often there were wild bursts of mutual laughter as one of us toppled onto the mats or staggered upright for a few spastic strides or merely managed—for the first time in weeks—to grasp a small beanbag and toss it into another gimp's lap, which was our game of Catch.

If our arms worked at all, we lifted small weights or worked what muscles were still in reach—two of the group spent days simply learning to hold a table fork in a paralyzed hand. Those of us with more luck restored contact with muscles that had seemed long gone, and we learned to "rearrange" the others as pliant dead meat. Those with paralyzed legs—and several others joined me in denying their paralysis—learned wheelchair skills to the fullest, including the mastery of hair-raising wheelies in the dangerous effort to climb those curbstones that still make most American cities such jungles of inaccessibility. We managed transfers from chair to bed with two-foot-long wood sliding-boards; and we learned, from constant drumming by our teachers, the absolute necessity to press ourselves up every few minutes on rigid arms and let fresh blood flow through to our butts—the main technique for preventing the pressure sores which quickly become the lifelong bane of quadriplegics who can't raise themselves.

Few sessions passed without my learning at least one skill, and soon I felt surprising new strength in my arms and chest—more upper-body strength than in my past life. Throughout that summer my chest size went from forty-two inches to forty-six, and my arms and wrists thickened proportionally. Best of all, the new skills produced in most of us a heady sense of control and choice. Those physical choices are obviously more limited than the almost limitless array that's offered to the able-bodied. But in time I was skilled enough in the homely detours and reinventions to put myself through almost all the motions I needed for the necessary work of my life. In theory I was even ready for renewed access to sexual love, though desire would hide out a good while longer. I've never known why.

The very fact of strict limitations soon had me tasting a fresh intensity of focus and pleasure in the strengths that were left me. I'll risk the claim that, from the time I left rehab, I've taken more pleasure than most adults ever come to know from my present eyesight, hearing and taste, from the stretches of my skin that still have feeling, and from my mind's new grip on patience—surely more pleasure than I'd known till now, and I've been a competent epicure. To be sure, for some three years after rehab, I'd still be seized more than once a day by the ravenous physical hunger to *stand*, to rise to my feet, unfold to my full height and look straight forward, not merely up. If you could have given me just one unimpeded stretch, a quarter hour to walk through my house and out to the trees, I'd have let you take my legs from the knee down as grisly compost for your houseplants or garden. But even that hunger has died away; and I live on now in my natural posture, the shape of the crooked lightning bolt on the skintight jersey of one of my childhood heroes, Captain Marvel.

But those claims pitch me ahead too fast, way past years of serious trouble. Back in my room on the rehab ward, I was trained in washing and dressing myself, chores that were slow as flight in a dream. I was given instruction in hauling my pants down for unassisted transfer to a toilet seat but there I failed. As a brief introduction to the problems of the lame, if you're an able-bodied man or a woman in trousers, attempt the chore. Sit parallel to a standard toilet, fully dressed in a narrow chair. Deny yourself the power to rise by even an inch. Now work your pants and underwear to below your knees. Now using only your hands and arms—*don't cheat with your legs; they're mere dead wood; don't try to press your weight on your feet*—slide or hop somehow from your chair to the toilet, complete your business without mishap, reverse the motion and redress yourself. All but impossible, if you're not a professional acrobat.

More helpfully I began to learn the techniques for managing what's known as a "compromised" bladder. Severe spinal injury almost always damages the nerves controlling bladder function. A minority of paraplegics and quads retain some control of the flow of urine— luckily I have—but even the luckiest of us generally fail to empty our bladders, and urinary infections are frequent until some program of intermittent or permanent sterile catheterization is established. In my case, soon after leaving rehab, I began to catheterize myself some six or seven times in the course of a twenty-four-hour day. Awkward and costly as the process is, if I follow my schedule regularly it reduces infections to a tolerable minimum—two or three per year. Each time the process consists of inserting a new sterile hard-plastic catheter, sixteen inches long, through the length of my penis, up the urethra, through the prostate and the bladder sphincter, then draining the urine into a small male-urinal which I empty into a commode (if I'm near one).

And while the process can sometimes result in internal cuts and subsequent infections, it also greatly reduces the risk of one of the steady concerns of gimp life—public mishap. The bowels of course bring their own awful problems, but a gimp makes his or her own arrangements through trial and error with those threats. Since the muscles that expel feces from the lower intestines are inactive in most of the paralyzed, some form of rubber-gloved manual removal is generally required. Whatever the individual gimp hits on for a workable method, he or she quickly becomes as familiar with his own piss and shit as any Paleolithic cave-dweller.

In the rehab kitchen I learned to dodge, if not entirely escape, the hazards of simple cooking. They lurk mainly in the risk of burning a body that's numb to heat—in my case, most of my trunk and lap and both my legs. I was even led by our game excursion-therapist to my old supermarket, the first such visit in more than a year. There I learned at least to ask bystanders to fetch me items from the higher shelves. At wheelchair level, stores mostly shelve such crucial items as dog food, toothpicks, charcoal briquettes and cases of beer.

Best of all as a culminating new skill, in the same sun-broiled parking lot where fifteen months ago I'd discovered my appalling inability to run, I proved to Wilkie my ability at moving unaided by means of the narrow wood transfer-board from the wheelchair to the driver's seat of my own car; then folding the chair, removing its wheels and stashing the parts in the back seat behind me. Driving with hand controls is a feat that defies every ingrained reflex for braking and the adjustment of speed; it was not included in my program's aims, and I wouldn't tackle it for two more years. But veteran that I was of so many forties and fifties films that charted the literal resurrection of bodies from war wounds, I felt for the first time, in that parking lot, the same sense of triumph that always flooded the ends of those stories. *Ah, make room for me!*—Marlon Brando at the end of *The*

Men wheels his own way from the gimp ward back into broad daylight.

Useful as those skills would prove in daily life, looking back I can see that by far the most important gain of the four weeks came in the intimate day-and-night contact with other people as hard up as I and often much worse. There were some twenty of us; and our range of damage included octogenarians and a young woman-dentist halted by strokes, a woman in late middle age who'd lost a leg to diabetes, an older woman whose breast cancer had moved to her spine and stalled her legs, a young woman who'd attempted to shoot herself through the heart but had hit her spinal cord, and a young man of Olympian physique whose wife (having caught him in the flagrant act with another woman) shot him through the spine and paralyzed his legs. There were likewise three high-school boys. One of them had spun out as he sped the car home to his father on a weekend night and found himself paraplegic in a cotton field. The other two boys had been flung head-first through windshields at ninety miles an hour and would never stand or think straight again. At the very still core of our tribe was the beautiful child we centered on—our tragic worst, a fourteen-year-old girl whose kid brother had accidentally leapt on her neck at a swimming party in celebration of their father's second marriage. By the time I left rehab, she could turn her head slightly and barely flex her thumbs; many months later I'd hear she was there still, little improved.

Among us all, there was only one who failed to rise to the steady and frequently painful work. He was one of the boys with traumatic brain injury, so he may not even have comprehended the point of the effort. He'd bellow his rage in our weight-lifting sessions; he'd curse the therapists and wet his pants in what seemed an active will to offend. Each of the others, however diminished, turned up at every session in the gym and at the three meals we shared in a common room, feeding ourselves or fed by members of a staff of salty but indomitable kindness.

I soon felt closest to the younger of the two boys with severe head damage. He was seventeen, had spent the last two years in several of the state's rehab centers, and could so far only use his feet to pull himself forward in a wheelchair. Yet his thinking seemed surprisingly normal for a boy his age. Only the uncontrolled wild range of pitches in his speaking voice betrayed a grave loss. Otherwise he met us with a good deal of wit, the will to help, and an adolescent boy's unceasing horniness. I was the frequent audience for a story he plainly enjoyed repeating—one female attendant in another rehab had given him at least one memorable session of penile massage and earned his undying boisterous thanks (his voice was incapable of whispering). And I knew he'd paid me a high compliment when he asked me to come to his room one night and sit beside him as the Miss Universe beauty pageant played itself out on color TV to his loud cries of joy and longing.

In time I came to like him so much that I inadvertently pained him. After dinner one evening I was lying on the bed in my room with the door shut. I heard a scratching at the door and, unable to rise fast, I called out "Come in."

Very slowly the door opened on my friend in his wheelchair. He dragged himself in, laboriously shut the door and backed up against it so that no one could join us. Then he faced me directly and said "Mr. Price, will you be mad with me if I tell you something?"

I said "No."

He said "You are my best friend now, so I don't want you to be mad with me—"

Puzzled, I again assured him.

And at last he took a long breath and said in his plunging and soaring highs and lows, "I like you very much, Mr. Price; but I don't like it when you *talk like me*."

I understood at once. I'd done it with others. From long exposure in childhood to my father's brilliant powers of mimicry, I'd acquired a kind of sympathetic unconscious tendency to mimic the accent and vocal rhythm, sometimes even the gestures and tics, of a person whose immediate company I was enjoying. So I must have at least once mimicked my young friend's uncontrollable voice, maybe in the course of our rowdy evening with Miss Universe. Quickly now I tried to explain and apologize—I'd tried to sound like him because he was my friend. Was that clear and believable?

He thought it through carefully, looking down. Then he faced me, nodded fiercely and said "All right"—his voice rose sharply. "Just don't *ever* do it again."

I vowed I wouldn't and I think I succeeded. Anyhow he never reproached me again, and our friendship flourished in the rest of the time we had together in that strange indoor island-world of badly sideswiped bodies and minds where no one among us could claim a prize for looks, skill, suffering or anything more than sheer endurance in the bared teeth of loss.

Yet however much our band of cripples may have resembled a swarming Hieronymus Bosch assortment of ludicrous damned souls in high torment, all but one of us grew in skill and self-reliance and above all in the raw appetite for more life. Exhaustion and laughter were our main pastimes as we worked through our days in standing contraptions and parallel bars, tossing our beanbags to one another across short spaces, laid out on the floor and challenged to haul ourselves into chairs, donning our steel and canvas prostheses that were more than Martian in their bizarre impracticality, and wetting or otherwise fouling our pants as we moaned with pain or roared at the sight of one another, in hilarious sympathy.

I managed to keep *Kate Vaiden* ticking, a few lines in the rare off-hours when there was usable energy left. They were also hours in which I dwelt on the steep and constant rise in a pain that had many times seemed as high as I could bear. Whatever the cause—and a constant stretching of scar tissue was unavoidable—the searing burn down the length of my spine and across my shoulders and the jolting static in both my legs only soared in intensity. Like most real agony, the pain afflicted more senses than one; it often shined and roared as it burned. More than once I panicked in the glare and noise. The morning after my first crisis, which a resident treated with useless morphine, I told my diagnosing neurologist that I had to find help. The calendar only records this response,

Pain is something they turn from in embarrassed impotence.

But three days later with no prior warning, an orderly came to roll me down to the Pain Clinic. After a long wait, flat on my back in a corridor, two doctors heard me out in separate interviews. One was a psychiatrist, one an anesthesiologist. When they joined to report their findings, they at least acknowledged that I wasn't insane. And for the first time yet from any physician, I heard the unvarnished news that's nonetheless crucial for any sufferer who hopes to live. According to them I had "central pain." My central nervous system—specifically my spinal cord—had taken massive damage from tumor, surgery and radiation; and that dense cable has proved, so far in medical history, entirely unforgiving of harm.

Then the doctors recommended a set of drugs, including the synthetic opiate methadone. Before I could mention an obvious concern with addiction, both men assured me that few patients with true central pain ever develop a physical dependence on narcotics, though methadone is generally considered more addictive than heroin. And the help of the Pain Clinic stopped there, where so many American physical problems are grounded by doctors who've blindly or willfully impoverished their humane intelligence—on prescription blanks. Neither of the pain specialists made any mention whatever of the proven survival techniques which at that instant were on hand only yards away from the Pain Clinic. And it would only be after two further pain-obsessed years that I finally learned, after making near-frantic pleas to my doctors, that lasting help was available—to me at least and in the same building as the Pain Clinic which offered me nothing but handsful of drugs that clouded my life for years to come.

For then however in the summer of 1985, the fruitless treadmill began—a narcotized life. Till I started withdrawal more than three years later on my own initiative, my daily intake of mind-altering drugs included amitriptyline (Elavil, one of the older antidepressants and one with some potential for relieving pain), tryptophan (an amino acid which may promote sleep) and the vaunted synthetic opiate methadone, which one of my streetwise companions in rehab called "doctor's heroin" and congratulated me for getting. My neurologist had already prescribed baclofen (Lioresal), a powerful relaxant to lessen the intense leg spasms that were still rising in frequency.

The cause of the spasticity which follows in the wake of so much paralysis is still poorly understood by doctors. What's startlingly clear though to anyone who experiences its arrival is the immediate fact that the spasms can greatly complicate movement. They tend to start some weeks or months after spinal trauma, and at first they tend to come as mild twitches that may be interpreted as signs of new life—the slow rewiring of broken circuits. A good doctor warns you to quash that hope; and fairly soon the spasms intensify in strength till, at frequent and unpredictable moments, they can seize a leg, thrust it out board-stiff and shake it wildly for as long as a minute. My own spasms have been less intense than some I've seen, but they've occasionally been strong enough to throw me out of my chair or off the shower stool. Despite the dangers however, spasticity has one advantage over the other condition available to the paralyzed, which is general flaccidity. By giving hard involuntary exercise to the leg muscles, the spasms preserve the health of tissue that otherwise withers and results in the stick-like legs of many polio survivors. My legs are stronger-looking now than ever before in my life, though they couldn't transport me one-eighth of an inch to avoid, say, a fire.

The first day after I took the new drugs, I noted in my calendar, "Very groggy but no appreciable pain relief." That paradoxical description would summarize my constant experience for two years to come—numerous drugs, continuous grogginesss, doctor-prescribed experiments with two external "pain-relieving" devices, and moment by moment barely touched pain. If I'd never stopped howling in all that time, would the neurology staff at Duke or the Pain Clinic have directed me to the no-cutting, no-drugging upper floors where the physiological behavior laboratory was located?

If I'd busied myself in Duke's large medical library, reading about my changing symptoms, would I have made my own discoveries and demanded to have the latest remedies? If, like my hypochondriac father, I'd become the anxious and always doubting haunter of an endless line of doctor's offices, would I eventually have found the medical help I needed at particular moments? Would I have got the available but deeply concealed or mysteriously withheld advice I needed on practical matters like diet, leg swelling with its ruin of the skin, mental stability and pain control? They're after all matters from which so many American doctors turn as apparent trivia. What if I'd not been deterred by the fire and ice—and severe damage—of radiation oncology and had simply returned to my original internist, the kind man who'd nonetheless brought me my hard diagnosis in a crammed hallway?

Before I agree to a charge of self-pity, idiocy or willful self-negligence, a seldom-made point may need repeating. Despite my years of residence in a university community where some of my friends were medical doctors of world-famed distinction, as a patient I was in most ways an entirely average floater in the crowded wake of disease and its aftermath. Any special interest I possessed as a patient was the result of the extraordinary size and intractability of my particular cancer. So like a vast majority of the millions who seek help for life-threatening trouble—and most human beings do at some time in their lives—I was plunged into degrees of pain and realistic depression that produced a dangerously passive state. In that psychic bog of helplessness, like most trapped sufferers, I was transfixed by the main sight in view—my undiminished physical pain. And in such a trance state, for that's what a heavily drugged life is, any personal crusade for sane alternate therapies was literally unthinkable to me. It was all I could do to focus my scarce strength and clarity on one main aim beyond plain endurance. That aim was somehow to work at a high pitch, day and night, on poems, plays, fiction, essays, whatever.

Wasn't I a patient at one of the world's great medical centers? In fact I was and in time I'd be thankful for the life that some of its staff would help me regain. But given the fact that—after one whole year of avoidance—I'd returned to the premises for a month's stay in rehab, wasn't I normal in assuming that if likely remedies existed I'd surely be sent straight toward them? Should I have abandoned mainstream medicine entirely and plowed an independent path toward, say, the alternate holistic practitioners whose ads in the local underground press ranged in tone from the faintly respectable to the outright fraudulent?

As I've said, superb alternate methods existed under the same roof with all the hard science and prescription blanks at Duke Hospital, as they do at most large medical centers. But the methods were never once mentioned to me, not by anyone—no doctor, nurse, orderly or physical therapist—not for twenty-four months after I'd described, as clearly as my verbal skills permitted, the nature and extent of my pain. Instead, in the technological paradise of medical America, I was left to sit and bear central pain with whatever resources my solitary mind could summon in its torpid drugged state. And that was the plight of a man who'd been lucky enough to acquire nineteen years of free education, a man with compassionate and decent doctor-friends and with a better-than-average lay knowledge of medicine. Imagine the fate of the millions less lucky and less well placed who are likewise struck with the same victim's mute passivity. Most of them live on sheer brute stamina, the body's dogged refusal to quit, till they die in blind torment.

When I'd completed rehab after twenty-six days, I went home feeling not only the Brando sense of triumph but also knowing that I now possessed hard skills for navigation. I was likewise equipped with a wheelchair tailored to my specifications, the memories of plain heroism and laughter on the faces of my ward mates, and of the generous care from nurses and therapists. Toward the end of the month, I'd also got a piece of what seemed good news. In the year since my initial treatment, a remarkable new machine had arrived in a few of the best American hospitals. It was the magnetic resonance imager which I've mentioned as being unavailable at Duke in the spring of '84. Eventually called the MRI, the imager is essentially a machine for accurate visualizations of the body's internal soft tissue, tissue which X rays cannot see in adequate detail.

Shaped like the immense long torpedo tube of a submarine, the MRI engulfs a live body in its narrow confines—a claustrophobe's nightmare. By means of a powerful magnet, it aligns the hydrogen atoms within individual cells and produces detailed pictures of the deep interior of the brain, the cord or whatever tissue needs inspection. Only after I'd benefited from its pictures did I learn that a friend from my graduate days at Oxford University was one of its inventors—George

Radda, a refugee from the suppressed Hungarian revolt of 1956.

The result of my own first two-and-a-half hours in the tube, on July 22nd '85, was delivered to me deadpan a whole week later by my neurologist on his usual very brief visit with a huddle of interns, all working hard to look glum as ashes. I noted that

Dr. X said my scan shows "no change" during the past thirteen months. . . . Felt buoyant all day.

The buoyance lasted a good while too. I was assuming, without further question, that "no change" meant "no new growth." I barely noticed till a few days later that it likewise meant "no apparent tumor reduction." Had all that vicious bombardment done nothing more than stall an advance?

With that to ponder as I left rehab, it also seemed I'd acquired one not-quite-new but worsening problem. As the gathering outcome of immobile legs and the pooling of lymph and other fluids in my lower extremities, the swelling of my legs and feet increased severely. I'd long since discarded all my old shoes; but the skin of my feet, in their waterlogged state, was now dangerously fragile. The least nick or scratch in sodden skin could take months to heal. The physical therapists and two physicians whom I consulted only recommended a strong diuretic. For a while I took it and urinated oceans of fluid but with no reduction of the grotesque swelling.

It would be two years before Pia, my sister-in-law, remarked that her neighbor with multiple sclerosis used a Jobst extremity pump for her legs. The pump consists of a small compressor which inflates a pair of thigh-length cloth boots and literally forces fluid from the legs back into the circulatory system. Since then I've generally spent an hour or two each day, lying down in the tight high boots with a small compressor raising the pressure to sixty pounds, then deflating and starting again—a process that keeps the swelling to a minimum and restores the skin to far better health. But that one remedy, courtesy of a family member, runs me far ahead.

5

Back home I watched Jeff Anderson and his fellow builders construct a permanent wheelchair ramp from my back door to the driveway. L-shaped and built to ideal specifications, the ramp sloped at an angle I could climb and descend on my own—so many ramps are steep-pitched slaloms, negotiable only with able-bodied help. And soon I began regular home workouts with an excellent new physical therapist, Deborah Hodges (Diana had returned to full-time work in pediatric therapy at Duke). Dan and I made a second good visit to Marcia and Paul at the shore; and once we were back at our separate desks, we plunged into our separate jobs.

On September 5th '85 I completed the writing of *Kate Vaiden*, a draft of her entire story at least. Through the next two weeks, I tinkered at minor but absorbing revisions; and on September 20th I typed page 394, the end of the final draft. My relief was immense. Now I had one more external object to show the friends I'd put off for so long, a sizable thing completed and polished after so many friends had thought I was dead. The next day Dan flew north to New York for his own earned rest and to pass the manuscript to my agent.

Jeff Anderson stayed with me, he and Lettie cooked

for me, and during that weekend they made me an offer of astonishing friendship. It was an offer that flowed from the main predicament I'd still refused to deal with. Even with my new strength and skills, there could be no question that a three-tiered house was a minefield to movement. I needed new quarters with wide doorways, vacant floor space to maneuver in and a sensible bathroom. Now with no hint to me, and certainly none *from* me, Jeff and Lettie had redrawn their plans for a house they planned to build on ten acres of woodland I'd sold them uphill behind me.

Their revised plan included a wing designed for me and the wheelchair; I'd live with them for the rest of my life. I thought long and happily about their gift. As it turned out, in calm discussion we ultimately made other choices. We would go on living with a hundred yards between us yet separate for now, but no one since the death of my parents had made me the offer of such a long commitment, and that fact alone would be as strong a prop as I'd have in the bone-rattling change that waited for me six months ahead.

Meanwhile I went on dragging myself several times a day down the parallel bars, telling myself that my right leg was strengthening. In the physical therapy sessions with Deborah, we'd work on learning the complex method of lurching hip-swings that permits some paras to walk upright with crutches and long-leg metal braces. But though she and I seldom expressed discouragement at my slow and maybe illusory progress, we gradually abandoned the notion of braces and moved back indoors to work at more realistic projects.

With regular vigorous kneading massage, in time Deborah broke up the thick foot of scar tissue down my spine; and with treatments by a small electric probe, applied to points along spinal nerves, she made brief inroads on the pain. Mostly we huffed and puffed on the floor in the usual trunk and arm exercises, heaving me in and out of the wheelchair. Since we quickly reached the apparent peak of my possible strength, the main good effect of continuing effort was probably psychic. I was doing something about myself and under the guidance of a benign professional who could laugh beside me through the tumbles and groans.

By early fall '85 anyhow, I was ready to make my first air trip since surgery. For more than a year I'd assumed that plane travel was all but impossible, but Dan made the necessary calls to discover that commercial airlines had long since learned how to handle the crippled with a minimum of risk and pain. On October 6th then we set off for Conway, Arkansas to begin rehearsals with Rosemary Henenberg, her staff and students at Hendrix College on the first production of *August Snow*, the play they'd commissioned eleven months before.

We stayed in a local motel in a room equipped for wheelchair use. In fact, for the only time in my experience the room was not merely accessible but was comically over-equipped. The bathroom was not only bristling with grab bars, the sink was not only open beneath to permit roll-unders; but overhead at various strategic locations in the bath and bedroom, trapeze bars hung on iron chains with lifting pulleys. The general effect was perhaps more suitable for a campus visit from the Marquis de Sade than a paraplegic playwright, but the equipment served its purpose.

And the experience further revealed that most American motels and hotels have at least one room they've designated as wheelchair accessible, though a visit will almost certainly show—even now after the passage of the well-meaning but so far toothless Act for Disabled Americans—that most such rooms have been designed by some vaguely well-intentioned but able-bodied planner with no clear sense of what's required by an actual human with paralyzed, or even weakened, limbs.

The correct grab bar, placed three inches to the left or right of where any gimp can tell you it should go, will prove worse than useless. Bathtubs seldom have usable chairs or benches, washbasins are often enclosed underneath (balking wheelchair approach), shaving mirrors are generally set well above wheelchair eye-level, bedside phones and lamps often prove unreachable by a supine gimp. Few accessible rooms have connecting doors to a second room where a friend or assistant might stay in easy reach. In adjoining rooms, with no internal connection, your only hope of rescue in the event of trouble lies in the telephone—one of the first things to fail in emergencies. And like most traveling gimps, I've more than once encountered, in otherwise fine metropolitan hotels, a perfectly equipped gimp-bathroom that lies just beyond a doorframe that's inches too narrow to admit a standard-width wheelchair.

Through the two weeks at Hendrix, rehearsals went like a lit powder trail. The cast was a winning set of young men and women dealing in earnest with themes they'd already met in their own lives. And in Rosemary Henenberg they and I had a director of quietly brilliant and warmly sly skills. Not only was I back in touch, after a long gap, with invigorating students; I was having for the first time in my career a playwright's ideal condition—the chance to write and revise on living actors. One of the subtlest actors, Eric Bailey, became in later years a valued friend; and in Rosemary's playwriting class, I met Rex Lisle, a fine writer who's befriended me steadily ever since.

The text of the play benefited in pace and clarity from each day's work, and another large gain came unbidden. Again I was reminded of a home truth that chronic-pain sufferers often forget—the fact that a thorough immersion in absorbing and, if possible, nonstop activity is far more narcotic than any drug. And the cast and company of *August Snow* politely but firmly demanded my full submergence in the task at hand. So I'd write all morning and afternoon (I was also writing poems again); then we'd rehearse till past midnight in the handsome Wilbur Mills Theater. Withal, the pain stayed with me, to be sure, making frequent lunges in hopes of my pity; but the job at hand kept my daytime focus well off the scalding drone.

At night a whole new set of hurdles loomed up before me, a siege of pertinent but terrifying nightmares. They may have been partly triggered by my continued stupefying battery of drugs—the simultaneous methadone, amitriptyline, tryptophan and baclofen combined to thrust me into morbid depths of unconsciousness the moment I shut my eyes each night. But it's probably truer to see the dreams as realistic options that my mind was running for possible futures in the time left to me. In any case, for a string of busy nights, my mind subjected me to utterly convincing scenes of total paralysis.

None of the dreams had a trace of plot. They were each as bald as any sudden confrontation with horror; and each was some visually lucid variation on a basic scene in which I was flat on my back in bed, staring toward the dim ceiling in sudden knowledge that I couldn't move, not even the smallest cell of my body.

Still sleeping, my mind would tell me to strain for the slightest gesture to break the lock—a shrug, a bent finger. I'd strain to try but I couldn't so much as blink my eyes. I was literally frozen, though sweat poured off me in the actual bed; and the fact that I never cried out and woke Dan suggests that my voice was likewise frozen.

Each time I'd wake in the dark room, soaked and wondering again if I was being warned and trained for such a life. Was this the *More* I'd heard of at Marcia's on another hard night more than a year ago? I could still after all be healed of cancer but go on freezing into full immobility as the aftereffects of radiation continued to kill off cell after indispensable cell (the effects of radiation on the body cease only with death). Bad as the dreams were, while they were on me, oddly they left no lingering dread. If anything, they let me see the worst, eye to eye. Shaken, my mind somehow chose calm as its morning response. So the general goodness of the trip was unspoiled, and I probably met with real luck in facing the threat of full paralysis away from home. My own quarters would at least be free of the aftershock of those awful sights.

And when we left for home in late October, with the play's premiere nearly three weeks away, I knew we'd try to return to Hendrix and see it performed—that hadn't been planned. I was also already feeling the ferment of numerous questions that the actors had asked about their characters. *Why did he do it? Why does she care? Will they manage to rescue a foundering marriage? Who will they be as time moves on?* They'd started me thinking of further lives for each of the people, though I had no plan yet to track the lives down.

On the next-to-last night of that second visit, in the same motel where I'd run the nightmares of total paralysis, I had the most startling dream I recall from my life till now. It saw me again, not as frozen but as literally swallowed, engulfed; and the following day I wrote it down plainly in the daybook of poems.

No jeweled hummingbird, no angel
Equals (much less passes) me.
I hang midair in a dim cathedral,
Poring slowly down faces of windows
Lit by setting sun outside—
Enormous roses, apostles, crowns;
A thousand tints of violet, green;
Then the face of God.
　　　　　　　　I prowl its hair,
Planes of a forehead prairie-wide;
Then dip past the cataract nose and lip.

The mouth springs open, an endless hole
That swallows me—the grandest bird.
I plunge down a throat more gorgeous than glass,
A luge-run paved in Byzantine mosaic,
Billion translucent gilded tiles—
All joy till I comprehend the goal,
Terminus waiting at Time's own end:
The heart of God, God's belly and vent.
Whelmed, doomed, I pray to stop.

No answer. On.

Insofar as the dream forecast new rounds of defeat and surrender, it proved prophetic, enacting its threat in under three months.

On the third day back at home from that first stay in Arkansas however, I unexpectedly found myself at the computer, beginning a play. To that point I'd had my word processor for more than a year but had continued writing my first drafts in longhand, then entering them on the computer every few days. But I'd yet to compose anything more than letters or notes directly on the computer screen. So I recall clearly the head of excitement as I sat down on October 23rd to make a few notes for a possible sequel to *August Snow* and, in under an hour, found myself at page nine of a new play, composed straight out in the green-lit letters of an almost embarrassingly eager machine. No sheepdog ever worked harder to please.

A quick week later, on October 30th, I had a first draft of the play that eventually became *Night Dance*—the characters from *August Snow* eight years on in their interlocking marriages, kinships and passionate bonds. The play had come at a speed I'd never experienced in any earlier long piece of work. I knew right off that the word processor, with the lights and allure of a video game, had played a big role in drawing the text out rapidly; and I glimpsed the prospect of working hereafter at exhilarating rates. I also recalled the universal proverb that "Things come in threes," and I wondered if a third play would dawn on me soon.

Meanwhile on November 8th Dan and I flew to Arkansas again for the final performances of *August Snow*. The play has been acted many times since, but no production that I've yet seen has surpassed that first in freshness and piercing youthful depth. No other actors, however well trained, have yet matched the sight of those young amateurs burning their intense candor and animal grace like all-but-lethal torches near us. At the closing-night party I told the company about the second play and gave them a quick rundown of the plot. They had still more questions about the fate and luck of their characters down through the decades to here and now.

So back home from that second trip, once I'd corrected galley proofs of *Kate Vaiden*, I started a third play on the computer; and it sped like the second. On December 17th I had a first draft called *Better Days*, the final piece in a full-length trilogy about one family in a single place from 1937 to 1974, the late years of the Great Depression through the war in Vietnam. They were people at the same time wise and foolish as the adults I loved or feared in my childhood and whom I'd steadily tried to become.

For a while the calendar took no notice of health or pain. It notes good hard work, the titles of video movies we watched, meetings with friends and a Thanksgiving flight with Dan to Mississippi to visit a friend I'd badly missed. Before I met her in 1955, Eudora Welty had meant as much to my early work as any living writer from anywhere; and the friendship which she'd given me so freely in my twenty-third year, as though to a practiced colleague in arms, had never flagged with the years that brought us oddly similar pits and ambushes. Together for a few fine autumn days in the landscape captured for good in her work, we could gauge the tolls we'd each paid out since our last meeting—my tolls to cancer, Eudora's to arthritis—but nothing impeded a quick resumption of the laughter we'd shared for thirty years. And those unmarred days in the presence of her stillness, with my sense of luck in sharing the company of a person with such huge powers of *watch*, renewed my awareness of the absolute worth of a single life that was sleeplessly merciless in what it saw, yet was finally tolerant of all our lives and had never denied its need of love from the time she'd been the tall wide-eyed girl who moved to this house in her early youth and stayed here, generous and hungry as ever for the humming current of human connection.

That safe spell of weeks ran on into Christmas '85, which stays in my mind as a last peaceful dream before a new nightmare. Dan's former girlfriend, Jennifer Beals, had sprung into notice two years before with her performance in the film *Flashdance*. Throughout Dan's early months with me, Jennifer would phone, all hours of the night, from wherever on Earth she'd reached on her travels in the wake of the film's world success. I'd answer at two or three a.m.; and there her mild voice would be—Japan, Rome, Denmark, the back of the moon. I'd yell to Dan; he'd often still be writing in the study or reading in his bedroom, and he and Jenn would talk half the night. So when Christmas neared and she, who by then was a student at Yale, was marooned exhausted and in flight from a bad relationship, we invited her down.

She came, her opulent Pre-Raphaelite beauty half-hid in jeans and sweatshirt, with funny gifts for us—palm-sized machines that, when pressed, would produce the sound of hundreds of wildly clapping hands: a canned ovation for the day's low moments. Outside, the weather was cold and gray; but the three of us huddled warm indoors for a few days that seemed like years on a raft— three humans from far-flung ages and homes, all of us beached on various rocks and a little hazy but live and glad till Jenn flew out on the 27th; and reality washed back, chin-deep and rising.

On December 29th '85 my calendar notes:

This week has seen a decided increase in back and leg pain, spasticity, and weakness in my right leg— now basically beyond any control.

And with that began the worst time of all. Just as I'd seemed well launched on a new chance at movement and work, I was—as that last dream had forecast precisely— swept into a long stretch of new dark tunneling.

In January '86 I returned for the first time since May '84 to teaching my annual semester at Duke, a course in the poetry of Milton and a seminar in narrative writing. I'd taught them both for many years, so I had no hard new ground to break. And with no prior request from me, President Brodie saw to it that the university took elaborate steps to ease my way—a rare response as many crippled workers know. They'd moved my office from the now-unreachable fourth floor of the library to the third floor of a building served by an elevator. They installed a new couch in my office for occasional rest, and they rebuilt the nearest men's toilet. After an edgy few days, I settled back into the second of the two kinds of work I'd wanted to do since adolescence—working through books and conversation, and through carefully examined imaginative writing, with interesting students.

Anyone who's never taught for long has failed to receive the peculiarly tough and steady dose of daily judgment which students readily provide. Other compensations are native to the trade. As an old teacher-friend of mine once said "Name three good reasons for teaching school—June, July and August." And despite my continuing notes on pain, the first five weeks of term went better than I could have hoped. Not only was I soon thriving again in the tight arena of class discussion, the normal exhaustion of such encounters was welcome in the after-hours at home. There was far less time to watch myself like a ticking bomb or a dying heart.

Still as my fifty-third birthday neared, this short poem appeared in the daybook—an omen.

Time is clearly no concern of the Great Watchmaker—
Keats, Mozart, Schubert, Anne Frank, James Dean;

My father strangled at a hale fifty-four,
Still working the ground at his feet (sweet laughter);

Me jackhammering my slow path, micron by micron
Toward my own dread: his early ghastly howling end.

But with surface calm I managed to face the near prospect of Dan's departure. Months earlier we'd calmly agreed that since he'd been with me more than a year, and since I seemed to be on a new plateau of mental and physical stability, then he must soon choose a date and leave. He'd got a grant from the Lyndhurst Foundation to continue his writing; and almost at random he'd got the idea of settling in Santa Fe, a town he'd seen only briefly. So he chose early February '86, and we worked toward that. Surely I'd find another live-in assistant in plenty of time.

Wrong. I was hoping not to be forced to hire a professional nurse or companion; but in all my tries at finding a friend or a former student who might want to live in a country house for a stretch of months and have free time for his own pursuits, I came up empty and full of foreboding. That was in spite of serious urging from an older friend that I contact the State Probation Department and hire a recent felon. When I showed slim enthusiasm for the risk, my friend said "Well, you could spend five hundred dollars on some psychological tests and know if you had a serious lemon."

In a tense close call, there was only a week of Dan's stay left when, on February 1st, a friend in Tennessee phoned and gave me the name of a first-year graduate student in classics at the University of North Carolina in

Chapel Hill, eight miles away. The student and I met at once, and he accepted my offer on the spot. He was Lawrence Wall from Selma, Alabama; and though it seemed the least likely nickname for a man of his interests, he responded by choice to "Bubba" Wall. He'd only just finished his B.A. degree at the University of the South in Sewanee; and when he moved in on February 7th, Dan was free to leave next morning. As an external marker of the change we were making, *Vanity Fair* published Dan's first essay—based on his meeting with Nadine Gordimer—the day he left.

I felt real sadness at watching him go. His undownable presence through seventeen months had literally carried my life across a bridge I might well not have crossed alone or with anyone else then known to me. We'd built a haphazard friendship between us that, now I could see, ran tall and deep. But I also shared some of the relief Dan must have felt in going on, a new sense of cleared space and fresh unpredictable air around me. For a short while to come, he and I would be friends whose faces summoned the memory of dire times. Meanwhile we'd correspond about our work.

The next afternoon, a bright warm Sunday, Lawrence had gone to Chapel Hill to collect more belongings; and I was writing letters at my desk. At a pause I leaned too far back in the wheelchair, and it rolled right over—no one's fault but mine. My head thudded hard on the floor; but once I recovered breath, I checked my limbs as far as I could see—no apparent blood. Good, my luck was holding. I extricated myself from the wheels, dragged myself across the rug to the desk, managed to reach the phone and called Jeff, who came from next door and lifted me. By then I was chuckling at the mental picture of my neat backward flip, and by the next morning the incident seemed so negligible that I failed to note it in the calendar. But toward the end of the next week, I noted

Back stiffness—and pain—very intense from 14th on.

On the 17th I received a mortgage check to begin the addition of an east wing to my house—a one-floor apartment for me and the wheelchair, designed by Jeff and consisting of a bedroom, a study, a sun porch and another small bedroom which I thought of as a "monk's cell" in case I'd eventually need a night nurse. But as Jeff and his colleagues broke ground and began to frame the new rooms, my mind and body only slid downward.

Doctors had asked me more than once to rate my pain on a scale from one to ten—*ten* being agony to the point of unconsciousness, *one* being a low-grade headache. And there'd been a few times when I claimed a *nine*, especially in the early days of rehab. A few days after the wheelchair roll though, I was privately rating my pain at a *ten*, then soon a *twelve*—all of it in my back, neck and shoulders. Since Lawrence was off in Chapel Hill at class all day, I'd found an affable Duke graduate student, Matthew Hearn, who'd stay with me during those hours. I hoped that he'd be free to do his own reading, but right off I threw him this bout of pain. On the tenth day after my wheelchair roll, for the first time yet, I couldn't sit up to slide out of bed. The pain was that ferocious and frightening. I couldn't even sit up to eat but was fed by Lawrence through a straw.

I called for Bill Price to stay with me that night. By eight the next morning, he'd convinced me that my need to see a doctor exceeded my dread of reentering the tunnel of full dependence on the choices of others. And since I couldn't transfer to the wheelchair, we had no choice but to call an ambulance. I'd never been hauled out of any house before, much less my own. The only time I'd known my family to need an ambulance was the day my hemorrhaging mother was hurried thirty miles to a hospital after she'd prematurely delivered a dead child—I was three years old and can picture it plainly still. Sick as she was, I thought I'd never see her again; but I lived to know I'd misunderstood the power of skilled humans to save her.

So now as two gentle medics lifted me, rolled my stretcher out the door and got me down the steep front steps, I thought I could hear again the same crack of doom. Now I'd be forced to concede to myself, and the few friends I'd told, that my mind had invented or misunderstood my dawn in Lake Kinnereth and the promise of healing—hours at a stretch, alone, I'd wonder how I'd waylaid the promise. My affirming friends had proved dead wrong about my living, and my native confidence was routed. I was thinking mainly *This cancer is alive again and racing to take me*. I'd never been righter. As the ambulance headed down my drive, I could see Jeff and his two fellow builders pause in their work on the pointless new east wing—surely I'd never last to use it.

I have no other memories of the day beyond the fact that Allan Friedman was away at a conference and that the strange neurosurgeon who saw me merely raised my dose of narcotic, adding another drug to "potentiate the methadone." Then he sent me home in mid-afternoon, again by ambulance. I don't have a calendar note to date it; but at roughly this time, I was also fitted with a new electric TENS unit (transcutaneous electrical nerve stimulation). It consisted of a cigarette-pack-sized box, with wires and two black rubber electrodes which were taped to the skin above my spine. In theory the unit would send out intermittent charges of energy to block the passage of pain impulses from my spine to my brain. But after months of daily use, I was forced to conclude that the unit was helpful—for me at least—only as a toy. The chance to fiddle with its buttons and knobs, increasing or lowering the transmitted charges, and endless experimentation with placement of the rubber patches gave me a brief sense of doing something with the pain. But any relief was barely detectable; and soon the unit joined my closet full of outgrown clothes and useless devices—a cane, a walker, a mammoth trunk-brace, long-leg splints, a deep-heat machine, heel protectors and a crowd of smaller and outrageously costly failures (all of them sold to me, or Blue Cross, at the extortionate rates that leave me hoping to be at Heaven-Gate the day the makers of "disabled aids" arrive to beg for admission).

"No relief," the calendar says for February 21st '86, the thirty-second anniversary of my father's cancer death. Then it goes blank. I was flat in bed, still at home, still unable to sit. And though Bill, Pia, Lawrence and the Andersons tended me closely, the pain only went on brilliantly finding new ways to grow till I couldn't so much as turn in bed, much less think of rising. Soon my head wouldn't lift from the pillow, and my only means of passing time were the bouts of sleep which the methadone brought me. So on February 27th the calendar says "Entered Duke Hospital for tests." That involved another ambulance ride—this time with Pia (Bill was away); her presence was calming.

I knew that I'd already missed a week of classes. An elaborately arranged effort to lecture to the students from my bed at home, on an amplified telephone connection, had proved impossible—I heard them; they couldn't hear me. But now they were off on spring break, a ten-day pause. If some ramshackle help could be found—drugs, numbing alcohol injections into spinal nerves, even the cutting of more nerve tracks—maybe I stood a chance of being up and ready by the time the students were back from Florida, Bermuda or skiing the planet Neptune. Then at least I could finish my promised term. That goal loomed big in all my next thoughts, almost bigger than the hope of survival.

Friedman heard my symptoms and said at once that I might well have cracked one or more vertebrae when the wheelchair rolled. Obvious as the connection sounded, it hadn't occurred to me. The fall had seemed near-comic at the time, and the pain had waited five days to start. But of course I was ready to believe in any cause but cancer. So I entered a whole new round of X rays—tomography and a new myelogram. Drugged as I was, I don't recall a second session in the MRI torpedo tube; but there may have been one.

I recall clearly though that all those days and wakeful nights were the summit of pain in my life till now. The one good memory of that whole stay in Duke Hospital was the constant kindness I received from nurses. From all my stays I recall no nurse—woman or man—who was less than helpful. My strongest memories though, and thanks, are for the calm black women who'd answer my calls in the predawn hours of this painful stay, when I needed help to turn in bed.

By something more than an accidental grace, more than most others, those women were able to blend their professional code with the oldest natural code of all—mere human connection, the simple looks and words that award a suffering creature his or her dignity. Not at all incidentally, they were the only persons in my recollection of my hospital stays who ever asked my opinion of my care—was I being treated well? What else did I need? Certainly no medical doctor ever asked. Many times since, I've thought that if I were ever to donate a work of art to Duke, I'd commission a realistic bronze statue of a black woman in a nurse's uniform and ask that it stand by the hospital door.

On March 1st I noted "A nadir of pain in the night"; then on the 3rd,

Friedman proposes further tumor surgery on 5 March. I decline, to the staff's incredulity.

All I recall Friedman telling me—once he'd studied the test results—was that, yes, I might well have cracked a vertebra; but he'd broken off so much vertebral bone two years before that he couldn't determine further damage with any real clarity. One thing was sure though—the tumor clearly was moving again, upward toward the base of my brain. He'd recently had encouraging results with a newly developed ultrasonic laser scalpel and was ready to try what had seemed impossible in June '84. No guarantee of course.

To be sure, the news was awful. But when I instantly declined his date of March 5th, I was not declining the principle of more surgery. I was focusing with a child's purity on finishing my one term of teaching. I was after all the heir of a father who was often unemployed in the Great Depression. If I dropped out now, I might never return; and no one would trust my word again. Even if I should want to return, surely the university would insist that—given my uncertainties—I retire on disability. I was likewise surely drug-controlled by methadone when I made the decision. I'd certainly had no trace of a hint that my employers were losing patience.

Friedman honored my choice as quickly as I made it— no hesitation, no attempt to dissuade me. *Right*. Say the word; he was ready when I was.

I said I'd see him when I'd read the last final exam from my Milton class; that would be late April.

I was back at home on March 10th, but pain kept me on in bed till the 18th. Then I managed to return to teaching—"much pain but I managed"—and I kept at it steadily with gradual improvements in pain and strength that had my hopes reviving briefly in an early spring. I almost never write on a Sunday; but on March 30th, Easter Sunday, with Lawrence away in Alabama and my friend Eric Rector staying with me, I sat on the porch in full sunlight and wrote a sketch of Eric in the daybook.

> *Permitted to write on this one Sunday*
> *Of all the year, I roll these two*
> *Uncertain hands (cold, twitching)*
> *Into flat frank sun, face east and draw*
> *The day's best sight—concave planes,*
> *Hid valleys, hot wells (two walnut eyes):*
> *Your resting face, consuming light.*

By April 12th though there were new realities. There's still no reliable means of measuring human pain; and it hardly seems likely that I was right when I felt pain rising by the literal day. Was there no ceiling on its power to climb; was I simply imagining the rise? I'll never know but one thing was sure; the pain was now accompanied by what I noted as "nausea and mental malaise." The nausea came as morning sickness, a daily case of the

134

retching dry heaves to start the day. The malaise consisted at first of dizziness whenever I tried to read, silently or aloud, for more than two minutes.

Months earlier the student literary magazine had asked me to give a spring reading from my work. On April 16th then, with numerous faces watching me in a bright auditorium, I was overcome with the certainty that I was babbling garbled nonsense, not even real words. But the faces before me seemed unruffled, and back home a tape recording proved to my astonishment that the hour had gone ahead smoothly. My sense of babbling was at most a delusion.

But in Milton class on April 17th, the last day of term, I was sure again of speaking fluent gibberish, something that felt like an awful bird-language. I pushed ahead with frequent checks of the students' faces for signs that my behavior was baffling. In particular I checked my friend, Dot Roberts, who was auditing the class. None of the students showed unusual concern. Dot was watching with her great dark eyes and seemed unruffled. Was I hallucinating their calm? Given my knowledge that by now the tumor was almost surely pressing on the base of my brain, such delusions of public humiliation came down as the hardest warning yet. They were fears as old as my first day of school nearly fifty years past.

Obsessed as I was with finishing the job, I had nowhere to turn for physical or mental help except to prayer and a few homemade meditation techniques. I'd given up imaging long months back as an unbelievable investment in the unseen; and prayer, after all those months, was threadbare. What could I say but *Over to you; brace me for it—whatever it is—and thanks for the interesting overtime?* I often said that much anyhow as I

135

dragged through ten days of term papers and final exams. With the dizziness that accompanied any reading of more than a few seconds, each paper took three times normal to finish. But finish I did, in pigheaded triumph.

Then I entered the neurosurgical ward of Duke Hospital on Sunday afternoon, April 27th '86—my fourth entrance there in two years. The calendar noted "A very calm night," and Monday says in a firm script

> 6:14 a.m. to surgery—Bill with me. Awake at 5:30 p.m. Apparently excellent results.

My only memory of waking is that Friedman stood above me in the thin-cream light of recovery rooms and said "Now work your hands for me."

Groggy as I was, I didn't recall that, all day long, he'd been cutting in the upper cervical reaches of my cord, at the base of the brain, a zone with zero margin for error since both hands and arms are worked from there. But I obeyed. I pulled my arms up out of the sheet and moved my fingers in childlike spider-gestures of menace. Everything worked, from the waist up at least and for the present.

Friedman smiled the broadest I'd yet seen and I slept again.

The next few days of the calendar show that "Bill's elated. . . . Friedman ebullient." What Friedman had found were three large cysts and a good deal of tumor in the cord above the hairline on my neck. He'd drained and permanently shunted the cysts. Then with the new scalpel, he'd removed the visible tumor for some inches downward. Now he proposed to pause for six months, then go back for another long session and remove the rest.

136

I'd never seen him really hopeful before, and I was more than ready to bank on his confidence. What I was still too grogged to consider was the uncanny timing. With all Friedman's skills, this rescue had come with the help of a new tool, a scalpel designed for the hairbreadth transactions of neural surgery. My latest crisis, had it come a few months earlier, might well have killed me.

This time I was home in just ten days, May 7th. But the high spirits that followed surgery had abruptly crashed into fresh hard ground. I was caught in the throes of a violent reaction to sudden withdrawal from the steroid given to brace me for surgery, my old enemy Decadron. For some chemical reason, the quick withdrawal had thrown me into panic attacks—the first of my life. They'd strike without warning or rational cause many times each day and night. My breath would shorten, my heart would race and I'd feel pure terror like nothing I'd known before. Something appalling was ready to happen. I had no idea what or how, but I knew it was only just out of sight and bearing down fast. When the panics were on me, I couldn't bear to be alone, even with the door open to a busy hall beyond me or back in my fine new apartment at home with Lawrence only yards away.

In a far too normal hospital procedure—the general rule of throwing chemicals at any fire—I was given powerful anti-anxiety drugs, Xanax and Valium. They only added spin to the panic, though I was too far gone in desperation to recognize the fact. So I was spinning hard for several days before Bill Price learned what I was taking. Then he told me that our mother had responded identically to Valium years back after a hysterectomy, when I lived in England. The intended calming action had reversed and crazed her briefly. Since I'd shared so many of her allergies throughout my life, I had at least a cause to blame.

But a quick withdrawal from all the anti-anxiety drugs had no immediate effect on my mind. Even at home I couldn't sleep alone without cold terror at unpredictable times in the night—if this sounds spoiled, believe me, you haven't known chemical panic. Bill and Lawrence alternated in sleeping ten yards from me on a cot in the new monk's cell. But the terrors stayed close at hand for a month, right through an unplanned return to the hospital on May 13th.

That hitch resulted from a stubborn urinary infection, the cause of death in most paras and quads before the advent of antibiotics in the mid 1940s. But as the fever slowly responded to intravenous antibiotics, the panic spells continued; and another more serious hitch appeared. My still-unhealed incision began to leak spinal fluid, a few drops at first—a fact incidentally that was not first noted by a doctor or nurse but by Pia Price, on a social visit. Apparently the tissues in my upper back had been impaired by radiation and were healing poorly. In my room on the ward, once Pia alerted the staff, a resident added a few more stitches to my fragile incision.

But the leak continued. At dawn on the 18th, I woke with my head in an actual pool of the straw-colored fluid; and later that morning, I was rolled back to surgery for another long day of anesthesia while Friedman replaced my original gut stitches with stronger nylon. That kept me in the hospital ten more days; and again at home the terrors continued, though I'd been off mind-drugs for many days.

In rare calm moments I still thought the panics were

138

spawned by chemicals, but soon I had a hard reason for rational fear. On two separate nights I woke to find my right hand completely paralyzed on the sheet beside me, not "asleep" from lying on it too long but entirely out of my control. Slowly both times the hand recovered strength and moved, but was I facing another round of *More?*

Maybe the panics were real warnings from a part of my mind that had proved foresighted more than once. Were they bald forecasts of quadriplegia? I tried to believe that my briefly dead hand was merely a passing response to swelling from the new nylon stitches, but those night glimpses of further loss surely fanned my terror. What does a middle-aged writer do with no hands? I could think of blind writers but no quadriplegics.

Again Lawrence slept nearby; and when the panics failed to ease, four months after his winter departure, Dan Voll offered to fly in from Santa Fe and help tide me over. I took the offer gladly. He came and stayed for nearly three weeks, in the monk's room. And the simplest way to define the grotesque strangeness of the time is to add that I felt no sense whatever of the self-absorption involved in overturning the lives of my friends. The calendar goes blank again for nearly two weeks.

But in slow time the fears receded, then vanished entirely. And my back healed enough to let me sit up longer and longer, though with new highs of pain, a slight new numbing of my fingertips and a curious absence of natural oil in the skin of my palms. A nerve that controlled secretion in my palms had apparently got nicked, a small price to pay for the huge gain. There were no further paralyzed hands in the night though. I noted the change in the first daybook poem for many weeks.

A whole quarter's silence—
Flesh-colored tunnel with sanguine walls,
No time to speak of pain or fear,
No extra breath (and no real
Fear: fear is the luxury
Two years behind me,
A bourgeois comfort like overstuffed chairs
Or flannel sheets and pain
More nearly a bore today
Than the acid agony that blanked all March).
So life, an apparent road ahead
With what seem trees and sky for walls
And natural light. So work. So this.

On June 27th Allan Friedman made his first visit to my home, a generous call to remove my stitches. And by June 30th I was healed sufficiently to take my first shower in two months (till now it had been very careful sponge baths). On July 3rd I noted "Life seems to begin again. A full work day." I was back full-time at the writing desk—poems and several essays I'd promised—and the work was coming at the same quick clip I'd known in the winter while writing plays.

On July 9th '86 *Kate Vaiden* was published; and soon a tide of favorable notices and sales poured in, the best reception I'd had for a novel in more than ten years. For a month I dealt with the raucous pillow-fight atmosphere that quickly brews round successful novels. Almost no reviewer disliked it. I recall only one, a New England woman who disapproved sternly of Kate as a person. A flock of interviewers flew in; and from their published stories, many lost friends learned of my recent history and some restored contact. But I resisted traveling to

New York to celebrate the renewed proof of life with my editor, my agent and other friends.

On August 8th I began what I hoped would be a new book. It returned to the lives of the man and woman in my first novel, Rosacoke and Wesley from A *Long and Happy Life*. They were well into middle age, still married, living in Raleigh; and each of them met a private blank wall early in the story. Wesley vanished from home—no warning, no address. Rosa was raped. Since I'd last dealt with her in my second novel, A *Generous Man* in 1966, I'd occasionally wondered if her and her husband's ongoing lives were interesting enough for another look; but I always concluded they were sadly becalmed in normal existence.

Now for the first time they seemed to be caught in watchable acts of interest to someone other than me; so I plowed on with them, daily and fast. I had some awareness that again I was plotting the course of lives parallel to mine—years of fairly smooth sailing in work and love, then shipwreck—but again the pleasure that came from the work was the pleasure of making something not *me*, lives profoundly different from mine and in most senses a lot more likable and compelling.

The only hitches came from outside my workplace. There were more fevered bouts with bladder infections that eventually yielded to antibiotics. More troublesome though, there were steadily escalating new highs of constant back and leg pain. After every surgical invasion, however successful in tumor removal, my spinal cord increased its howling as new scar tissue formed and pressed on already crushed nerves. Pain I'd have rated as an *eight* or *nine* only months ago now seemed to double, then double again. Were my nerves truly that inventive in their newly ruined state, or was I going more than a little mad?

But when I reentered Duke Hospital on October 2nd '86 for the third actual raid on the tumor—the one that I hoped would see the eel's last segments gone forever—I had nearly half the new novel behind me; and I felt nowhere near the level of dread I'd known before previous surgeries. When Friedman called in to see me that evening, he seemed both cheerful and genuinely hopeful. To be sure, the permission form he brought still listed my dangers as further paralysis and death. Yet the calendar noted "an extremely calm evening." Among current patients I was the ward's oldest hand by now; and though I knew old hands could die as easily as new, I took mild pleasure in my veteran status. The next day's schedule felt like routine, as it proved to be.

To surgery at 6:30 a.m., Bill with me. Awake at 5:35. To Intensive Care at 7—again with Bill. Friedman claims great satisfaction—"We're way ahead of the game." Flat-supine but a very restful night.

When I was lucid enough to talk, Friedman repeated his patent delight in removing so much more tumor tissue. In lieu of a guaranteed cancer-free bill, but with a good deal less of his old caution, he repeated that we were in far better shape than we might have been. I noted his first-time use of the *we* and began comprehending the stake he'd had in my case from the start when he'd foreseen a thoroughly dark outcome. By now I could see that his satisfaction was far more nearly that of a well-meant fellow creature than a self-respecting virtuoso; and I wished I'd had the self-possession two years before to see his shy phone calls for what they were—

offers of friendship, not grist for his files. From the start I'd liked his selective candor and his lone-wolf independence in a place where so many travel with gaggles of worshipful acolyte-interns, but a combination of fear and my own instinct for lone ventures had kept me from taking the fullness he offered.

Four days after surgery I got the first copies of my new book of poems, *The Laws of Ice*, most of them written in this new life. Meanwhile, friends had trooped to my room with food, flowers, balloons, ribald gifts and plentiful laughter. This time I insisted on withdrawing gradually from the surgical steroid. There were no further panic attacks; and at the end of that first week, I noted "a kind of stunned beatitude." But the second week brought another torn-incision crisis—a big clear splotch of spinal fluid on my pillow one morning—and my blood pressure spiked. After a watchful night and next day though, the threat receded; and I recorded the literal truth, "I haven't been happier or more grateful for years."

I was mellowing past all reason toward the skittish visits from fledgling neurologists (who always approached as gingerly as if I'd ignite at any false move) and the trainee-kamikaze young neurosurgeons (who frowned in offended pain at my using actual technical terms for my body and its problems). I could now enjoy rifling their magic box of jargon and gestures; I was stealing their amulets and hair-nail fetishes and grinning at their subsequent unease. I half beamed on the few nurses and orderlies who conducted personal business by my open door at rock-concert volume, day or night.

I even saw the frozen oncologist again. One morning as I lay in my room, a skittish resident from radiation oncology knocked and entered. He asked if I remembered Dr. Z, my oncologist. When I said that I did, he asked if I'd like to see him again. Our last meeting had been in August '84, more than two years past. I saw no reason for a meeting now; but sure, why not?—I was riding high. Radiation oncology was in a separate building, some quarter-hour's trip away. I specified that Dr. Z was welcome to drop by; I wouldn't be stretchered to his gruesome surroundings. When the resident left, I assumed I might get a visit in a day or two.

But ten seconds later Dr. Z walked in, with no buffer troops. No smile, no handshake, no expressed pleasure in the surgical outcome. He wanted only to say that these surgeries, in spring and fall, had shown that indeed my five weeks of radiation had slowed the tumor considerably.

I thanked him for the news and, when he left promptly, I couldn't help grinning. In the past thirty months, I'd spent more than two months—sixty-seven days—in Duke Hospital. Most of those days had been more than bleak. But when I went home on November 16th, I noted a feeling I couldn't have entertained three weeks before—"A very oddly, memorably enjoyable hospitalization." At least another round in our war—mine and Friedman's with the awful and resourceful eel—had gone our way.

Since I've dealt unsparingly but fairly, I think, with one radiation oncologist, I owe at least a few words here on what I think I and any other patient might have expected to receive from him and from all other doctors, whether the doctors are more than well paid, as they often are, or whether they work in the grimmest of charity wards. I understand the lamentably drastic limits of their training (the continued assumption that they'll work on machines, not sentient creatures); I'm aware of their burdens in large hospitals or private offices, their frequent long hours and the potential psychic drains of their contact with anxious, pained or depressed human beings. I likewise recall, and without nostalgic glow, the less technologically sophisticated but generally more humane doctors of my childhood and youth—doctors with the legendary "bedside manner."

Those nonstop doctors were men and women who, in their willingness to visit patients' homes, had agreed to expose themselves to the context of patients' lives—the rooms they lived their precious lives in, the beds in which they'd expressed their love and bred their children. In my experience, those doctors never indulged in false consolation (they had after all few effective drugs); but the depth of understanding that they gained by submitting themselves to the lives of their patients—as opposed to demanding that their patients come to them, however painfully—gave them a far better chance of meeting the sick as their equals, their human kinsmen, not as victim-supplicants broiled in institutional light and the dehumanizing air of all hospitals known to me.

The vastly improved technology of modern medicine obviously requires that the seriously threatened patient come to the cumbersome machinery; most of it cannot come to him. But surely it's more than incumbent on the doctor to know the nature of the toll he or she has exacted from a fellow creature—someone in pain or fear—in forcing that move from the safety of home to the faceless threat of hospital hallways. And surely a doctor should be expected to share—and to offer at all appropriate hours—the skills we expect of a teacher, a fireman, a priest, a cop, the neighborhood milkman or the dog-pound manager.

Those are merely the skills of human sympathy, the skills for letting another creature know that his or her concern is honored and valued and that, whether a cure is likely or not, all possible efforts will be expended to achieve that aim or to ease incurable agony toward its welcome end. Such skills are not rare in the natural world. What else but the urge to use and perfect such skills on other human beings in need could drive a man or woman into medicine? What but a massive failure to recognize one's stunted emotions before they blunder against live tissue—that and an avid taste for money and power? And having blundered on other creatures, how can the blunderer not attempt to change? Is he or she legally blind as well? Maybe we have the right to demand that such a flawed practitioner display a warning on the office door or the starched lab coat, like those on other dangerous bets—*Expert technician. Expect no more. The quality of your life and death are your concern.*

Four days after I reached home again at the end of that third bout of tumor removal, I worked a near-full day and set a new speed that I'd only increase as poems and essays moved ahead and as plans for continuing the new novel warmed. A month and three days after the surgery, Friedman came again to my house and pulled the stitches so that showers and fuller movement could start. By December 9th I was back at the novel; and though the usual rise of post-operative pain surged higher, later that month I confirmed my hope for more than a modest lease on life by purchasing, from Ansel Adams' son, a handsome print of his father's photograph "Moonrise, Hernandez, New Mexico." In its wide compass of an entire village, sunset strikes a clutch of graves as it likewise touches an adobe church and a low line of houses that seem for the moment to stand a chance of guarding feasible lives beneath the frail moon that rises beyond them past the Blood of Christ mountains, the Sangre de Cristo under bright snow.

6

By January 8th '87 when classes began, I was ready to teach—again a large discussion class in Milton's poetry and a small seminar in narrative writing. The following day Eric Rector arrived from a stock-exchange job in California to succeed Lawrence as my assistant. Eric had studied poetry and prose writing with me in the early eighties and had helped me for short stints when Dan or Lawrence was on vacation. But for the past year he'd lived with his fiancée in California and worked in the San Francisco stock exchange. When I'd mentioned to him in a November phone call from the hospital that my full-time job would open early in the new year, he accepted at once to my great relief—I explicitly spoke of it now as a job. He committed himself for a year's tenure and rearranged his life to cross the continent (his fiancée would stay in California; they'd marry in the spring of '88).

Three days after Eric settled in and began to supply his excellent cooking—a main source of pleasure for the numb but the cause of frequent calorie disasters and further pounds—I learned that *Kate Vaiden* had won the National Book Critics Circle Award. While I've always felt that awards in the arts are all but meaninglessly random, I was glad at least that this one had come from hard-core readers with minimal patience. And I recalled with some bemusement an old remark of Truman Capote's, "Prizes are dumb but if they're gonna have em, I want em all eventually." I dodged the chance to fly to New York for the presentation. I was still unable to thread my mind through the hectic red-eye of Manhattan life.

It was an unusually cold winter for us in central North Carolina. There were frequent snow and ice storms, and at home there were power and heat failures through my term at Duke. Wheelchairs are comically reckless or useless on ice; so to keep my teaching obligations, Eric often wound up carrying me in his arms like a big parade-balloon of a child over long, otherwise impassable stretches. Unprecedented as the weather was in my lifetime, it had a peculiar serenity to it; and the poem I wrote a whole year later in memory of those oddly safe times with Eric preserves that feeling.

> *A whole day of sleet and just at dusk*
> *The power fails. We're left to face*
> *A frigid night with only the warmth*
> *Of a squat woodstove for thirteen rooms.*
>
> *And I with a fever and all the hours*
> *Of no way to read, watch a movie or type*
> *(Sob for Fate's inveterate fool);*
> *So I watch the jagged blade of an oil lamp*
>
> *And try to mime the altitudinous*
> *Thought of a monk winging a mind*
> *Blank as ultimate Buddha at simply a wall.*
> *An eon turns, I pass the first stars,*
> *They vanish behind me. And home at dawn,*
> *Even my name is unseen smoke.*

But classes went well, I felt no serious exhaustion, and the only complaints in the calendar notch further rounds of pain.

Grotesquely high pain. . . . Most severe pain since last year at this time—significant?

In March a spring-break visit to Eudora in Mississippi was sapped by what the calendar notes as

Extreme pain, unease, depression. Should we leave here at once?

I phoned Friedman to see if the pain might signal trouble—should I rush back and see him? He said "Stay put" so we lasted out a rocky week and drove with Eudora to the vast Civil War battlefield on the heights above the Mississippi River at Vicksburg; but we canceled plans to push on to coastal Alabama and visit Thomas McGuane, whom I'd met in Key West years before and whose work—as different from mine as anyone's—I'd always admired.

From then on, the spring and most of the summer of '87 were one long fling at the end of a tether of pain and the monomaniacal self-focus, self-pity, that pain eventually clutches to itself. For all the recent surgical success, my work had gone on being the main rescue from internal diversions; and somehow through the soaring pain, work went on holding firm beneath me. I'd managed to finish the novel *Good Hearts* in February. I'd met my classes, which provided their usual alternate absorption. And on March 15th I could tell the calendar "Today I have lived as long as my father" (he died at fifty-four years and six weeks). On the morning of the 15th, I glimpsed again outside in the pond that same blue heron who'd paid me winter visits for years, and the two events joined in a daybook poem addressed to my father.

> Given. Today I exceed your life
> By an extra day of gray warm rain;
>
> And there just now through glass on the air,
> My heron soars in to work the pond—
>
> "Symbol of longevity" here this year
> Long past his usual winter stay
>
> Despite two snows and his mythic age:
> Tall slate-blue spirit, never leave.

With Eric's cooking, we led a calm but pleasant social life; and an MRI scan that Friedman ordered in late March showed no signs of new tumor growth. The day he called with that good news was the first occasion when he, or anyone else in my hearing, mentioned that biofeedback training would bear investigation soon on the chance that it might give me some pain relief. With no real confidence in one more gamble, I ignored the suggestion and worked on through till the end of classes with steady notes on my one obsession.

Terrific—almost comic!—pain. . . . Astronomical pain. . . . Pain, numbness, malaise, and depression spiral up relentlessly.

Why didn't I move on Friedman's suggestion of biofeedback till late that spring, nearly three years after my first surgery and the onset of pain? First, despite

Friedman's recent success inside my cord, I was still more than dubious that anyone at Duke Hospital could help me, not with pain. They'd failed so steadily in that department. And since it seemed that my cancer dread could sensibly begin to fade for a while, did some new appetite for tension demand that I wallow awhile in masochism?

There'd been moments, earlier on, of somber enjoyment in hearing my friends mint words like *courage* and *heroism* for me. Was I reluctant now to risk the loss of "heroic" stature? It had been a welcome novelty for the old ex-playground butterfingers, the man who'd never gone to war. My later talks with chronic-pain veterans have strongly suggested that, yes, there's a vicious and strong temptation to nurture the hurt we wail about. The hurting has so nearly *become* us—become the whole core of our present self—that the thought of finally dismissing it from us feels scarily like desertion or killing.

So I suspect I'd become accustomed to soaking in a long-familiar misery and was frightened of change, even to risk finding help, though since I seldom mentioned my mania to anyone but Eric and my brother, I wasn't seeking wide praise for martyrdom. These facts anyhow are firm in my memory—the pain was high and all-pervading from neck to feet; it generally peaked in blinding storms late in the day if I was tired. It intensified in conditions of low barometric pressure; and for dozens of other mysterious reasons, by now it had seized frank control of my mind, my moods and my treatment of friends. Patience had ebbed to its lowest reach.

Shortly before I visited the biofeedback laboratory at Duke, one week proved pivotal in my life—the first week of June '87 and the third anniversary of my first surgery. On June 6th after two excruciating days in bed, I phoned

Friedman in desperation and pled for any help he knew of—the severing of all remaining spinal pain tracks or whatever it took to bring relief. I was still on a high dose of methadone that kept me groggy, devastating my short-term memory in return for no help; and I still occasionally fiddled with the useless electric TENS unit, but my mind was in the worst trouble yet.

I'd never shown Friedman such raw despair, and the calendar notes that he told me "The problem is dead nerves." He went on to explain the phenomenon of phantom pain where the brain, alarmed that information from a limb is failing to arrive, somehow projects intense pain to hover in or above the silent place (everyone's heard of the soldier who lost a leg years ago but still feels pain in the absent foot). Friedman then suggested that as a first step I begin taking amitriptyline again, initially low doses of the antidepressant with some potential for pain relief. Since I'd abandoned the drug as ineffective in the summer of '85, I had no real hopes for it now.

But on the night of June 6th, I took the first twenty-five-milligram tablet; and the following night I recorded this remarkable change:

> Drowsy but an immediate improvement—psychic at least! Pain hasn't dramatically diminished, but I feel removed to a new perspective—to the safe side-lines, watching the central situation at a cooler distance. And all on 25 mg. of a drug that hadn't helped me before! Not credible surely but it lasted till bedtime.

At no earlier point had any remedy—chemical, mechanical or psychic—produced such results.

152

Was the change in any way caused by the drug? As a rule tricyclic antidepressants take several weeks to exert their effects, if any; and a significant change overnight seems most unlikely. More credibly, maybe my mind was ready after so long to jolt up out of its leaden masochism and to dim the pointless alarm it was sounding for serious damage that could never be repaired. Or was this a further external healing, as uncanny as the dawn in Kinnereth and merely triggered by a few milligrams of a chemical that played no more effective role than, say, the mud that Jesus made with spit and smeared on a blind man's eyes to restore him? In any case I wasn't about to stare a beautiful gift horse in the mouth.

I felt tons lighter and, before I could crash again, my biofeedback training began. Quickly, with guidance from Francis Keefe and Betty Wolfe in a lab at Duke, I worked to stabilize the gain of June 7th. The blinking lights and beeps of their monitors, when attached to various parts of my body, soon taught me to contact parts of myself over which I'd never had direct control. Then they taught me simple feats of concentration which—again with electrodes taped to my body, blinking response— would demonstrate the quick effects of focused thought on pain and tension in any part.

Soon those same skills were helping my mind relent in its settled horror at pain and then to tolerate, if not quench, the flames. A few sessions later I was able to perform minor swami-type wonders such as raising the temperature in one of my hands by as much as eight degrees over the other, and with no aid whatever but focused thought. Astounding as it is to watch the red gauge record a rapid differential in temperature between your two hands, it's not a rare or difficult feat. I managed it after the third or fourth try; and any number of more practiced people can raise the temperature, say, in one finger and reduce it in the adjacent finger.

I likewise learned to relax tense fibers in my shoulders and neck. Those muscles would quickly bind into knots after only a few press-ups in my wheelchair, and the daily hours of work at my desk would hardly ease the compacted tension. Now I could pause, shut my eyes, think calmly and in thirty seconds be free of that pain. After a month of such sessions—one hour a week, with practice at home—Keefe and Wolfe observed that since I was fairly adept at concentration (pain victims are virtual geniuses at it, not to speak of writers), why not move on now to hypnosis?

So on July 17th '87, I met for the first time with Patrick Logue in the dim and creepy underground quarters of the Duke Department of Psychiatry. Logue was, among other things, one of the department's hypnotists and was often engaged in working with victims of repressed traumatic memory, phobias and addictions. Our initial meeting was mostly devoted to a discussion of my ongoing symptoms and to Logue's at first rather puzzling inquiries about any fears that I might have of the physical world—fears of water, heights, falling and so on.

I confessed to a fear of heights.

Next he asked me to describe some pleasant experience I'd had in the out-of-doors.

I sketched a day's boating on the Rogue River in Oregon some years back.

Then Logue dimmed the room; and with calm fluency and a trim eloquence, he led me through my first hypnotic induction since a single experience at age fifteen when my high-school biology teacher attempted hypnosis on our entire class but found only two of us susceptible. Briskly, with words and tone only, Logue brought me through a gentle descent from a tranquil sky with harmless clouds to the surface of an untroubled deep lake, then down through its waters to a hole in its floor, then down an elevator (floor-numbers flashing), down a long set of stairs (Logue tactfully spoke of my floating down them, no runaway wheelchair), then a sunlit breakout onto my old Oregon river-run—near total peace.

I followed him through the surreal plunge like a tranquilized rock, entirely trusting. And once I was in the same safe place I'd reached at the end of my day on the river, Logue spoke the real spell. In a clear grave voice, he said "The mind controls the body. All that's perceived by the body is perceived in the mind. If there's some part of your body of which you're more conscious than you wish to be, imagine that part as a shape. Now extend that shape toward the horizon till it's only a point of light." He took a long pause. "In your mind there's a rotary switch. Attach that switch to the point of light. Now turn the switch until the light fades and all but disappears."

I obeyed him with ease, first seeing my back and legs in the shape of a bent tuning fork; then extending that fork toward the far horizon, then hooking the rotary switch in my brain to the point of light, then dimming it out. A moment's pause in the sudden darkness, then—at Logue's calm beckoning—the equally brisk but still peaceful climb back up to daily consciousness at his slow count of three.

Awake, I felt an immediate and almost scary kind of physical relief, as if I'd snorted a sizable line of some illegal drug more potent than any I'd known till now. I wasn't addled or dizzy in the least; but I instantly knew I was free in a way I'd never felt before in my life, surely not for a moment of the past three years. The pain was still unquestionably in me; but as with the few milligrams of amitriptyline, it seemed contained and watched from a distance by my new self-possessed mind and eased body.

Logue had said that, with luck, I might expect a twenty percent relief from pain after each session; the relief might last for several hours. My calendar shows that the relief from my first induction lasted till seven o'clock in the evening, nearly three hours. As our more or less identical weekly sessions continued through July and August, the value and duration of relief only grew. And soon Logue gave me a tape of the guiding monologue he'd tailored for me, fifteen minutes of the quiet talk I've condensed above.

At home I'd disconnect the phone, seat myself comfortably, shut my eyes and respond to the tape two or three times a day. I used it especially when the pain blared up in volume or when I encountered some new frustration. In no more than a week of course I'd memorized the monologue, though the sound of Logue's voice and the skill of his guidance never grew boring, as repetitive listening so often does. Then, and only when Logue suggested, I began to practice weaning myself from his beckoning voice and working the ease in my own silent but watchful mind. If, on my own, I never quite went as deeply down as his voice could take me, I generally managed an intense new calm.

In under a month Logue felt I was ready to proceed alone; and for a few weeks, I continued working with both his tape and my lone concentrations. Again I tended to revert to his taped voice when I was tired or in need of undemanding company. But the spell had worked from the day he began; and within a few weeks of work-

ing at home, I began to discover that—for pain control—
I no longer needed the tape or even the quarter-hour
silent run-throughs in my own mind.

Within that limited stretch of biofeedback and hypnosis, no more than eight weeks, I'd grown essentially
free from pain. Not free from its constant presence in my
body—it roars on still, round the clock every day, in my
back and legs and across my shoulders—but free from
any real notice of it or concern for its presence, not to
speak of the dread and the idiot regimen it forced upon
me through three long years. And to be true to present
reality, I can honestly say that now still, six years after
approaching my mind for the help it could give, in an
average sixteen-hour day, I'm conscious of being dis-
turbed by pain for maybe a total of a quarter hour—in
scattered minutes, here and there, at this job or that.

Such lucky oblivion is plainly dependent on my occu-
pying my mind fairly steadily with other concerns. If you
ask me to rate my pain on the one-to-ten scale at any
moment, I'll quickly turn inward, watch the height of the
blaze and give you a number somewhere between, say,
seven and *nine*—almost never lower. But it's you who've
made me watch the fire and gauge it. Left alone with my
body and mind, I'm no more focused on pain's existence
than you'll be focused on the word *hippopotamus* at any
moment unless I tell you not to think the word *hippopotamus* in the next thirty seconds. If however you're
presently free of chronic pain, and I could instantly
transfer mine to you in all its savagery from neck to toe, I
think I'm realistic in saying that you'd lay yourself flat
instantly and beg to be hauled to a hospital, fast.

Even now, especially in the night, I'll awake to a level
of pain in my back that's like nothing so much as my

157

wound reopened and barbed-wire laces tearing at the inmost quick of the flesh and sending great licks of fire down my legs. Well over half my time now though, when I notice the pain, I see it on the far horizon of consciousness like the mute demonstration of a force from which I'm as safe as I generally am from the distant sun. Like the sun, my native pain burns there beyond me with an ignorant loyal heat, but I know I must never import it again to where I actually live and work. I must never conspire again with its aim to ground me entirely. I must *feel* it as real but not *suffer* from it, just as I understand that the dog desires to sleep beside me in bed but his nearness is no longer feasible.

More, I must ration all situations that offer pain a chance to return for more than short visits. Those dangerous gateways are moments of exhaustion, a sudden powerlessness to roll through some doorway or up a ludicrously steep gimp ramp, sudden outbursts of anger, self-pity or private responses to certain foods and drinks (salt, for which I have a normal craving, sizzles in my back and legs for hours after a spree). Yet odd as it sounds, in tranquil moments I sometimes approach the pain itself or lure it toward me for a bracing reminder, a quick and quickly ended surrender to its undimmed core.

What could have happened in three summer months of '87 that has freed me till now almost entirely from a savage form of literal enslavement? I've suggested that, from the first small dose of amitriptyline on June 6th, my mind was finally ready to shut the gates on a long ordeal. And only my mind could have chosen that moment since the whole ordeal was after all caused by my mind, the source and site of all human feeling. But like most human minds, my own was programmed from birth and reinforced in the cradle with the certainty that *Pain means trouble*—a finger's burned, a knife has cut me, stop everything and tend to both the wound and its cause; then the pain will relent.

In the case of my own brand of central pain, as with so many kinds of chronic pain, the mind's outrage is simply misplaced. With all its powers, my mind can make no significant physical amends to me for the permanent wreckage done to my spine in the course of three surgeries, a surgical repair-job and more than a month of spinal radiation. The causes are past yet the panicked alarm continues to blare. The mind's only hope for sanity then is to shut down the useless but frantic circuits and look elsewhere for ease and continuance. In the summer of '87, my mind was finally ready for that action. With the addition of biofeedback to my final readiness to free myself, I'd reached the handholds of self-control. With the added pleasure of hypnotic trances, which proved as accessible for me as they do for some eighty percent of those seeking professional guidance, I completed a round of full attention to my mind's deep need. It had desperately needed to hear and believe that the unending stream of neural alarm meant nothing now. The need had been filled. Now my mind understood that *The harm is done. It cannot be repaired; pain signifies nothing. Begin to ignore it.*

Outrageous as my pain was and brutal as its three-year tyranny proved, I well know that thousands have hotter masters entrenched in their skulls—physical pain from physical damage—so I take great care to pull rank on no one. And it's been a good while since I looked at my able-bodied friends and thought *My load is heavier than yours.* While I'm aware that my solution might prove of no use to another pain veteran, I've discussed it with many and know that some have already invented their own form of it to make real gains against the blind clamor of chronic pain.

From long reading in the lives of others less lucky than I, and from years of watching not only myself but a few close friends in agony, I think I can say that almost any degree of physical pain can be borne. And not only borne but literally displaced from the actual center of a human life and then ignored. I can make that claim because I'm convinced that all pain has one huge design on us—to rule our minds—and therefore that the secret of living with pain is wanting hard to throw it out of central control, then finding the sane means to work that steady mental combination of distancing and coexistence.

No easy task, God knows—or does he? Yet for me it was finished in a matter of weeks. Finished for now at least. Just as I never attempt to rival another's pain, I likewise never forget both my own crazed past and the threat contained in two cautionary lines from Shakespeare's *King Lear*:

> *The worst is not*
> *So long as we can say 'This is the worst.'*

At the actual worst, presumably, we'll be mute as rocks. Or howling, wordless, or humming nonsensical hymns to any conceivable helper.

That summer of '87 brought more compensations. In the midst of the formal hypnosis sessions, I finished *Full Moon*, the first draft of a play commissioned by the Duke drama program. And I wrote well ahead on two separate books that were, I'm sure, pried from me by hypnosis. Each was deeply rooted in memory, and memory was a faculty I'd thought much about in the weeks of working with Patrick Logue. In my sessions with him, though we never attempted to recover buried scenes of my past, we talked of someday attempting regressions. At the end of one session, we even ran through a quick exercise in which he led me, question by question, through the apartment building in which I lived with my parents when I was three. In instant replies I turned up a string of specific details which I'd long since forgot—or had just invented. Logue thought they might well be true memories. We went no further, then or since; but again I think that some never-sleeping zone of my mind heard me declare an important interest in a valuable source of buried memory.

So as it had learned to distance my pain without conscious urging, my mind now began—without my prodding and surely for healing needs of its own—to reclaim lost stretches of my childhood and youth. From the first my memory was eager to bring out detailed memories of the faces and actions of kin and friends who'd given so much of their time and substance to see me grow and eventually stand more or less on my own. By the end of summer I was inundated in memory. The work came fast; and by late August I'd finished a draft of a novel that flowed from my life in the summer of '53. That was a time when I'd worked as a counselor in a boys' camp in the Blue Ridge Mountains. For a quick ten weeks in that pure wilderness, I'd been as happy as the young animal I truly was, on the edge of manhood. And the novel that resulted nearly forty years later in my home office, with trees and a pond in reach of my window, would later be published as *The Tongues of Angels*. By year's end also I'd all but completed a memoir of my childhood and youth, called *Clear Pictures*. No previous books had tumbled from me at such a high clip of speed and pleasure. It was all I could do to type out the words before they log-jammed back in my mind, though once they were out I let them cool for later revision.

With the upper hand I'd recently got over pain and self-pity, I'd been slowly reducing my dosage of the narcotic methadone. I'd known from the first that the drug gave me little relief, if any. I'd watched it put me to sleep many times in the midst of meals or conversations. I'd realized that I could watch a video film with full attention, then wonder five minutes later what film I'd seen—I'd have forgot, not just the title but the subject as well. Yet I'd accepted such stupefaction and had wolfed the drug down for two main reasons. My doctors said it was the best they could offer; and I needed some hard instrument to cling to, some palpable proof I was acting at least to fight my pain. I've mentioned that the doctors in the Duke Pain Clinic had predicted in '85 that, despite the addictive potential of the drug and the high doses I'd be taking, I'd escape addiction. That far, they were right. When I told Friedman of my hope to quit, he advised me to step-down slowly; and he predicted that the final few milligrams of the drug would prove hardest to surrender. He said he'd be glad to bring me in for hospital care if the last days of withdrawal proved too difficult.

So beginning in July '87, over several weeks I went from a daily high of eighty milligrams to a trivial five. In the slow withdrawal, I met with no serious mental pangs or physical panic. But before I'd convinced myself that the pain was truly routed, my determination flinched; and I stepped back up to a pointless ten milligrams. I hovered at that token dosage till April '88 when I quit for good, with only a few nights of crawling sensations under my skin and a puzzling urge to extend my arms in the air above me and flex my fingers. I'd long since repaired my short-term memory and my tendency to doze, but total freedom from my opiate companion proved even more rewarding than I'd hoped.

By August '87 I was ready to trust the summer's gains and to act upon them in yet another way. Eric and I took the next opportunity and made my first flight north in four years. We didn't quite tackle full-blast Manhattan, but we came as near as Newark Airport where we were met and driven up the Hudson to the Thayer Hotel in the town of West Point. Despite its nearness to the army's prime academy, with a clientele that must include many wounded veterans, the Thayer's wheelchair facilities included forced rides in the stinking garbage elevator, an absence of ramps at all crucial points—including a steep row of unramped steps to the only dining room—and hilariously impossible toilets.

But a few miles off, on the grounds of the Storm King School, the remarkable Chicago theater company called Steppenwolf was in residence for a week of workshops. They'd shown interest in producing my *New Music* trilogy; and in the course of the workshops, the company read straight through my three plays—five hours long and a revelation, coming as it did from actors as good as Joan Allen, Moira Harris and John Malkovich. While the company eventually requested surprisingly conventional revisions that I declined to make, the stint helped me shape the plays for their successful premiere at the Cleveland Play House in '89 and for many subsequent performances round the country. And by making me brush Manhattan that closely, it finally assured me of the feasibility of regular social and working visits to the city itself.

The only cloud on the late months of '87 was again my difficulty in finding an assistant to succeed Eric Rector in January when he'd complete his year of help. But as I searched for Eric's successor, I was quickly reminded that—outside large American cities—there are very slim chances of finding congenial full-time care of the sort I needed and will always need. Television and the press retail daily horror stories of crazed companions, ranging from the smiling Tar Heel Strangler to the mild-mannered thief who pawns the spoons. But despite my contact with a large pool of candidates at the university, I'd so far resisted a search through the student body. Necessity soon convinced me that the scruple was pointless.

As Eric began his withdrawal however, Dan Voll was showing signs of wanting to move from Santa Fe back to his old home—Rockford, Illinois where he had a commission to write a play for the local Equity theater. By phone we spoke of the possibility of his making the move in two stages. He'd pause with me till I found good help; then he'd push on to Rockford. I suspected that, though he had several options, Dan felt some need to watch his investment in me at its new pitch of health. When he finally called to make the commitment, I could sense his ambivalence in returning to the scene of so much hardship; but caught in a bind, I was more than relieved to accept his offer. In any case by Christmas '87, Dan said he'd come to Durham and fill in with me from Eric's departure till early May. By then I was gambling that I'd have found a recent Duke graduate to sign on for twelve months.

So between January and May '88, Dan and I had a further chance to expand our friendship in an easier time, with none of the harrowing alarms of our old round.

Again we worked at opposite ends of the house on our own writing errands. He shopped and cooked as before, drove me to campus and participated in my writing seminar. The seminar proved unusually lively because of his seasoned help with a group of excellent students and because of an impulsive choice I made.

I hadn't written a short story since the publication of my second volume of stories, *Permanent Errors*, in 1970. And though I'd often been asked by editors, I'd really made no efforts to write more short fiction. The state of my knowledge and need in those years called for longer stretches of prose—novels and plays. And maybe the numerous poems of the time absorbed all shorter bursts of energy. Now eighteen years later, I found myself thoroughly cornered when I heard my voice tell the new class that I'd write beside them as a full-fledged contributor. Each time they owed the group a story, I'd owe a story of the same length and theme.

Years earlier, when I was barely older than the students, I'd worked at similar commitments to them. Now that I was silvered, seated and only a little younger than their grandfathers, this new round of students eyed me warily. Whatever else, my offer was spanking new to them; and students distrust any breach of routine. *Does this codger honestly think we'll say what we think of his work? Who'll be first to commit career-suicide and tell the teacher his latest story stinks?*

We wrote short narratives through our early meetings. The subjects were mostly suggested by me in the annual effort to reclaim the narrative instincts of a new small group whose notion of *story* has been fed to them, not by the tribal taleteller or within a family circle but by that baleful baby-sitter—the television set. So the first responses of young Americans here at the end of the twentieth century, when asked to write stories, are not to produce stories of the sort my generation wrote (we'd tended to take close looks at the power of home and family). However innocent they may be of life outside the rumpus room, American students now are prone to offer you emotionless stories of war or havoc in outer space. If they're at all prepared to tackle human feeling, they're likely to present in grudging prose either a pair of lovers or fellow loiterers so minimally noted as to have all the life and magnetism of blank typing paper; or if they aim for vigor and interest, they'll tack down a neat little plot for a competent made-for-television movie—a normal situation, then a lurid disruption, then a last-minute rescue with justice prevailing.

My first and last effort is to convince such barren-looking minds that, one by one, they're the sole caretakers of an already deep and unique store of emotional information and intimate response. They're the world's authorities, unless they've been phenomenally inattentive or brain-pulped by television, on their own line of sight and what that vision has banked in their minds. Whatever's in those unique personal storage rooms will almost always prove interesting anyhow if not world-arresting.

As I'd expected with this new class, their initial responses were cagey—*Who's this creep?* But as we moved toward finding individual themes for longer stories, and as I laid my tail on the block each time they did, they began to trust my request for candor. Finally, I think, most of them gave me as much by way of honesty as I gave them. Nobody wants or can use bald judgment, however precise. And by the end of term, I had a long story, "The Foreseeable Future." It watches a man who literally dies in the Allied invasion of Hitler's Europe,

June '44. Though he's resuscitated by battlefield medics and sent home to Raleigh after months of treatment, physically intact, he faces the bewildering task of learning to live a second life in the midst of the scenes of his buried past, the beautiful countryside of east Carolina.

My students barely spoke of the story's likeness to any problem that I might have faced in recent years, but they plainly glimpsed what I'd invested in such an invention. And convinced as I've been through the years of the value of measured truthful confession with students, I told them more than their diffidence asked me. The story was partly an allegory, however distant, of my own death and resurrection. That much of a naked risk on my part and the students' discovery of how to coach me through a few narrow straits made up an eventual reward for most of us.

By telling me when my private emotion was failing to reach them, they gave me all the help I could use. And in time I got short stretches of their ruthless candor. What they got, I hope, was one sane view at least of how live fiction can work its way into strangers' minds and how all else is likely to be both lethally boring and useless to humans. Better still for me, I'd also found a useful prod for writing more stories and a give-and-take forum for writing them in. Ever since, I've worked as a student in each of my writing classes.

Early that spring of '88, Dan managed at last to convince me that I needed an accessible car. With unusable feet, and an adamant refusal to install hand controls, I hadn't driven since the '84 surgery and was clinging to a small able-bodied Mazda that required awkward transfers from wheelchair to car seat, then cumbersome breakdowns and stashings of the chair. But now with a long list of other concessions to gimphood behind me, I was ready to abandon one last refusal to yield to irreversible change. Dan and I investigated the local sources for van conversion; and we'd almost ordered a full-sized van with the classic, noisy and unnerving platform-hoist when Dan discovered an ad in a helpful magazine to which a friend of mine had recently given me a subscription, *Paraplegia News*.

The ad announced a new company called Independent Mobility Systems in Farmington, New Mexico. They deplored as much as I the unnecessary awkwardness of full-sized vans, and they claimed to refit small Dodge vans with lowered floors and automatic sloping ramps. At the time they seemed the only company in America that offered such simplicity and convenience. The van in the ad looked ideal for me but would it work? A reconnaissance trip to New Mexico wasn't out of the question. But Dan bargained hard by phone, and soon a new van was trucked cross-country on two-week approval with the understanding that I'd pay return freight if we decided against it.

The company proved to be so eager for an introduction to East Coast business that two of its officials flew in to demonstrate their product for me. And the day it arrived, it proved near-perfect—I bought it at once. With Dan riding shotgun, I began to practice the six-ring circus of hand-control driving on weekends in the huge empty parking lot of Blue Cross Insurance, five miles from home. After a few frustrated weeks, I admitted that my old driving-nerves were refusing to learn a new complex skill (gas and brakes are worked on a single hand-lever that defies old reflexes—pull down for gas, press floorward for brakes and steer only with your other free hand). I gladly chose to retire from the wheel and leave all driving to my assistants. But the new access to easy riding opened another long-shut window for me.

So when Dan moved on again in early May '88, he left me in better shape than I'd been in for a four-year stretch lined with hurdles and traps. Not only was my cancer in a state of rout at the very least, but my home quarters were handy and pleasant; and I'd entered on what's been an ongoing line of uncanny good luck—the annual finding of a new assistant, generally fresh from spring commencement at Duke and committed to spending a year at the job of assisting me with personal chores, running the house, cooking and joining me on the road for the bristling baffles of airports and cities and the hair-raising labyrinths of most hotels.

The fourth assistant was David Lang, who'd just completed an A.B. in English and was ready to spend a year helping me and focusing on the music he hoped to write. He'd also declared himself game for an opening-out of my homebound routines, and I threw him a wide curve the week he arrived. We flew north for my first visit to Manhattan since I'd last been there in April '84 to hear Leontyne Price in *La Forza del Destino*. The destiny which Verdi portrayed so darkly had splurged itself fairly forcefully with me since those last hours in the darkened Met. Leontyne had retired from the blighted lives of romantic heroines and devoted herself to the concert stage. And I faced a city I'd loved since boyhood, seated now and hardly able to dodge the standard-issue muggers and geeks.

It was publication time for my novel *Good Hearts*. That provided a chance to see old friends at Atheneum, the house that had published all my books, and to thank them for the long-distance help so many members of the firm had sent me. It was also annual induction time at the American Academy and Institute of Arts and Letters (which since has simplified itself by voting the Institute out of existence and merging all members into the Academy). As a guest on several occasions, I'd first attended that pleasantly somnolent occasion in the spring of '62, just after publishing A *Long and Happy Life*.

From the balcony that year, I'd watched Eudora Welty present the gold medal for fiction to William Faulkner. The microphone had been set for Eudora's rangy height. When Faulkner stepped up in his short trim body, to read an acceptance, he failed to lower the mike and so spoke well below its range, in total inaudibility. At the end of the ceremony, he wandered offstage like an idle boy, determined not to smile; and he never seemed to appear at the reception. But late in the day, when I saw him in sunlight outside the building, his thick hair glittered a startling white; and I sensed somehow he couldn't last long. He was only sixty-four years old, but that would be the only time I saw him—two months later he was dead. In that same place, though, ten years later I met a writer whose long stories are a match for any I know in the whole reach of fiction—Tolstoy, Chekhov and Faulkner included. Katherine Anne Porter was in her eighties and forced to sit, but her small face still wore the elegant force that burned like the fuse of a perfect and world-menacing bomb in such stories as "Pale Horse, Pale Rider" and "Noon Wine."

In the same building then in May '88, I met for the first and final time a writer I'd come to admire very highly—Raymond Carver, whose late short stories place him firmly with the form's great masters, of any century. He was inducted beside me that day, a tall heavyset man who sought me out in the pre-lunch mob, bent down to me with a smiling grace surprising for his bulk and confided that he'd followed my work since his undergraduate days in Washington and that now he too was living with cancer. Not for long in his case. Once home, I wrote him with thanks and praise. He answered me warmly at the end of June, with the hard news that cancer had moved from his lung to his brain. At the end of the letter, he said

Do, please, continue to send your healing thoughts in this direction. —And I, too, look forward to our next meeting, and in less crowded rooms, yes.

I sent him the thoughts and reread his great stories, "Cathedral" and "A Small Good Thing." He died in August with heroic care from his wife, Tess Gallagher, the distinguished poet. If indeed Ray and I meet again, I'm fairly certain the rooms will prove less crowded; if any writer earned a new life with words and courage, it was Raymond Carver.

On that same visit, for the first time, my joints and muscles learned something a pedestrian can mostly ignore—the grueling ruin of the sidewalks and streets in a city I thought I'd known like my hand. To discover how hostile the pavement is to wheelchairs was by then no surprise. But in the four years since my last visit, the whole of New York had hit a skid of physical and psychic decay that's left it more than ever a wallowing moribund monster whose sickness is plainly past human solution, barring total destruction and a fresh beginning.

Forced to move at the height of a seated man, I likewise met full-on a brutally multiplied population of the dazed and homeless. Upright as I'd been for five decades,

I'd been able to share King Lear's neglect of the raw-
bone human misery that huddles beneath us. Reduced
to its eye level now as the homeless lay and crouched on
sidewalks—and meeting their fuming gaze as a standing
walker seldom does—I comprehended more than before
Lear's insight on the storm-swept heath.

> Poor naked wretches, wheresoe'er you are,
> That bide the pelting of this pitiless storm,
> How shall your houseless heads and unfed sides,
> Your looped and windowed raggedness, defend you
> From seasons such as these? O, I have ta'en
> Too little care of this! Take physic, pomp;
> Expose thyself to feel what wretches feel. . . .

With all that newness, still the full week was a last
confirmation that after four subterranean years I'd really
come through to the other side of my old life and was
certified now as a new thing—certified by a city that
shows a minimal mercy and by the friends I'd gone without for four long years: a new man who nonetheless bore
enough likeness to their former friend to permit resumption of dialogue.

I came home primed to complete the memoir *Clear
Pictures* and to travel more—a reading that summer in
Richmond, Virginia and further trips to Asheville and
Atlanta. Friends from Asheville drove us out to the abandoned site of Camp Sequoyah where I've mentioned
working at age twenty. The return was meant to prime
my recollections for a final draft of *The Tongues of
Angels*, and it served the purpose richly. Though most of
the buildings were in decay, the site was much as I'd left
it in '53; and more memories of my ten weeks there, with

two sets of campers to guard night and day, returned
with startling clarity when I found, on the eaves of my
rotting old cabin, the plaque on which I'd woodburned
all their names and mine.

> 1953—Reynolds Price, Counselor—
> Paul Auston, Jim Avary,
> Ed Grimsley, Buddy McKenzie,
> Tommy Moore, Raiford Baxley,
> Terry Brookshire, George Harrell,
> Jonathan Lindsay, Lester Shepherd.
> Ten-week campers: Bill Barrington
> And Randy Floyd.*

For whatever reason, the place and the time were a clear
platform where I could watch a plain summation of who
I'd been in the years behind me, where I'd gone and who
I was now. The grinning black-haired twenty-year-old
(weighed down with a boy's desires and hopes) and the
grizzled man at fifty-five (unburdened of pointless
dreams and fears) met for an instant—in the pine-slab
room in the midst of abandoned squirrel nests and the
ghosts of boys, now men themselves—and agreed to
part. A moment later when I left the collapsing cabin in
the arms of friends, I knew I'd left one ghost behind—a
likable but now quite useless remnant of who I'd been.

Then in Atlanta, David and I joined Kathryn Walker,
who'd performed so memorably in my television play *Private Contentment*, and her husband James Taylor, the
composer and singer. James was playing a pair of outdoor
concerts in Chastain Park. We'd met in the fall of '87

---

* The names are quoted from a poem about the visit—"An Afterlife"
on page 206.

when the Taylors had asked me to join them in Chapel Hill for James's concert in the packed Dean Dome. I'd quickly declined, not having entered that big a crowd for more than three years; but when James made easy arrangements for me, I'd gone with Eric and enjoyed myself. From then on we visited each other often. The Taylors' attentive unstinting friendship and contagious energy went a long way toward easing my further return to a venturesome life; and the fact that each of us worked together was an ongoing pleasure—Kathryn and I have given readings in New York and Cambridge; James and I have written two songs, "Copperline" and "New Hymn," both of which he's recorded.

By the end of September '88, I'd got the results of two new MRIs that Friedman ordered by way of safety. The first scan looked normal; but we tried it again, with injected dye to enhance contrasts for better detection of abnormal tissue. There were no new symptoms; and after studying all the images, even Friedman's ingrained caution let him say that there were no signs of return from the tumor, nearly two years after my last surgery. He did say though that he sensed we'd "have to deal with it yet."

I took the risk and said I bet against him.

He said "Well then I hope you win."

With that much assurance behind me, and with continued relief both from pain and the fear of ambush, I joined fully in the first production that fall by Duke students of the play they'd commissioned from me, *Full Moon*. While not as intense or probing a time as the weeks with *August Snow* in Arkansas, again a cast of smart young actors and two good directors helped me understand and strengthen a play that's gone on to have its own life around the country.

In early December we visited Washington and Lee University in Lexington, Virginia where I read in memory of my friend James Boatwright. Jim had finally succumbed to AIDS just two months before. In the face of the palpable sadness of his absence from a town where he'd taught so memorably for two decades, it was strangely rousing to be again on that elegant campus in its calm valley ringed with mountains and to see again the friends who'd surrounded mine and Jim's friendship for so many years when we were all young, and sickness or death were guests we'd not planned to welcome at the feast, and when Jim himself with his hungry mind seemed likely to outlive earnest me by decades.

The final lines of a poem I'd written the night of his death, when a mutual friend phoned with the news, seemed suddenly broad in their paradox.

> *Sail far, kind*
> *Ancient luckless boy.*

Jim with his haplessly open heart was a hole in the air of a hot late-September night. I, whom he'd so often railed at for worry, was back in his old place, stove-up but stoked with Jim's old fuels, work and friendship—a live man on the far side of at least one disaster.

Awhile before, hunting illustrations for *Clear Pictures*, I'd also written a daybook poem that was triggered by sorting the family pictures—more than a hundred years of kinsmen buried in shoeboxes, albums and drawers. The poem is called "The Rack"; and I'll let it stand, toward the end here now, for the balance of what I've done and felt in the years since 1989.

Weeks of threshing the family photos,
Gleaning faces to feed a memoir—
I start each day expecting sadness:
The thousand captive grinning eyes,
Long since blind in red-clay graves.
I find no fear on any mouth
But frank displays of a taste for time
As unassuaged as an alley drunk's
For dollar wine.
                    To have watched each one
From my own start, and now to set
Their secret down for a world to watch
And own and judge—More life. Bring it on:
A gift as big as any yet
From whatever unseen hand endows me
And stakes me too on the desert rack
That will parch me soon as dry as they—
A random ghost, all face, no voice
But maybe these lines.

Given my morning at Lake Kinnereth, my recent liberation from pain, and the ongoing steady stream of work, was I meant to see an external pattern in my new life—a forced descent into hot hellfire, a brief promise in the vision of healing, years of *More*, and now this rescue (however temporary) for life and work? However hairbreadth the rescues were, however unlikely the endless line of care from friends and strangers, the long disaster could all of course have been some meaningless falling-domino chain of events. And if it was more—a fate intended and overseen by a force beyond me—who was I to attempt a precise map of the dark terrain? Only a blissed-out TV Bible hustler would dare reduce that weight of mystery to a trail of tea-leaves spelling a read-able usable message.

So I've always stopped short of thinking I know all that happened to me or that I can lean on the shape of my future in any degree of certainty—if a further round of *More* starts tomorrow, I could hope to deal with it head-on, both eyes open and a minimum of howling this time. Having owned up to so much caution though about any meaning for what I've lasted through, I need to add that no one raised in my parents' world (and taught by their endless magnanimity) can doubt for long that the path ahead, seen from a tall enough height, will form at least a compelling figure, a clear intentional design, of use to others.

7

Was it disaster—all that time from my slapped-down sandal in spring '84 through the four years till I reentered life as a new contraption, inside and out? Is it still disaster, these ten years later? Numerous mouths and pairs of eyes have been, and still are, ready to tell me Yes every week. Very often occasional acquaintances will corner me on campus or at a party, then lean to my ear and ask how I am. When I tell them truthfully "Fine," their faces will crouch in solemn concern; and they'll say "No, *really*. How *are* you?" I'll give them a skull-grin to cover my amusement at the common eagerness of so many otherwise decent souls to see a fellow creature buried.

My amusement flows also from their hint that they know I'm hoarding a tragic secret to which they have an intimate right. They plainly believe that any chink in the normal human armor is a road down which all the curious are free to stream. That brand of assault is especially common now in politically correct middle-class America where the socially and physically gimped are crowned with a misplaced, thoroughly unwanted beatitude—the blessings of sainthood are mostly appalling as they've always been.

Physicians, in their admirable Greek and Latin mode, speak of a "catastrophic" illness. The Greek word *catastrophe* means an *overturning*, an *upending*—a system disarranged past reassembly, all signals reversed. The list of common catastrophes that wait for a final chance at each of us is virtually endless; and it now receives unimagined additions almost by the week from a viral kingdom that begins to hint at the chance of its ultimate victory over us, through cunning and patience.

Birth disasters, unstoppable cancers, disorders of the blood and lymph, external wounds to flesh and bone, those devastations in which the body turns on itself and eats its own substance, the mind's estrangement, the still irreparable disconnection of electrical service to major parts—each of a throng of catastrophes is as common as influenza or migraine, and so far I've missed a great many blows aimed at me; but I took this big one.

So *disaster* then, yes, for me for a while—great chunks of four years. *Catastrophe* surely, a literally upended life with all parts strewn and some of the most urgent parts lost for good, within and without. But if I were called on to value honestly my present life beside my past—the years from 1933 till '84 against the years after—I'd have to say that, despite an enjoyable fifty-year start, these recent years since full catastrophe have gone still better. They've brought more in and sent more out—more love and care, more knowledge and patience, more work in less time.

How self-deluding, self-serving, is that? Why do physically damaged people so often meet the world with clear bright eyes and what seem unjustified or lunatic smiles? Have some few layers of our minds burned off, leaving us dulled to the shocks of life, the actual state of our devastation? Or are we merely displaying a normal animal pleasure in being at least alive and breathing, not out-ward bound to the dark unknown or anxious for some illusory safety, some guarantee we know to be ludicrous?

Maybe I'd answer a partial Yes to all such questions. Though there's no "we" of course in the damaged world—the possible array of damage is too vast—I can risk a few observations at least that have proved true for me, through much of the time, and that may prove use-ful to someone else who's faced with a sudden blank wall in life and who may care to hear them, for companion-ship if nothing more.

I take the risk for one main reason that I've mentioned earlier—friends and strangers have asked me to add my recollections to the very slim row of sane printed matter which comes from the far side of catastrophe, the dim other side of that high wall that effectively shuts disaster off from the unfazed world. I've known what they mean. I shared their frustration for some fellow-words to con-sume in those weeks after radiation in '84 when I finally recovered the will to read and searched around me for any book, essay or sentence that might speak directly to the hole I was in—anything more useful than crackpot guides to healing or death, impossibly complex starva-tion diets, alfalfa pills and karmic tune-ups. In that deep trough I needed companions more than prayers or potions that had worked for another. But nothing turned up in my own library, apart from short stretches of the Bible, or in all the would-be helpful books that friends sent to me on every subject from crystals and macrobiot-ic cooking through cheerful wheelchair tours of Europe and the rules for a last will and testament.

Most of the books were either telling me why I had cancer—the utterly unproved claim again that I'd some-how brought it home in self-loathing—or they blithely prescribed in minute detail how to cure any tumor with moon-rock dust and beetle-wing ointment. Or they cheerfully told me what kind of deal I should offer God in hopes of the maximum chance at salvage—*I give you two good legs, the power of feeling from the soles of my feet on up to my nipples, control of numerous internal organs, and acceptance of pain like an acid bath with no letup. For that, you'll kindly permit me to crawl in and gorge my face by the television for however many minutes or years you can spare from your big store of eternity.*

I needed to read some story that paralleled, at whatever distance, my unfolding bafflement—some honest report from a similar war, with a final list of hard facts learned and offered unvarnished—but again I never found it. Admitted, there are richly useful methods, like the twelve-step program of Alcoholics Anonymous, for reversing long years of self-abuse. And the scathing self-disciplines of some religious sects have turned weak souls into flaming martyrs singing in the yawning teeth of Hell. But nobody known to me in America, or on the shady backside of Pluto, is presently offering useful instruction in how to absorb the staggering but not-quite-lethal blow of a fist that ends your former life and offers you nothing by way of a new life that you can begin to think of wanting, though you clearly have to go on feeding your gimped-up body and roofing the space above your bed.

So after ten years at what seems a job that means to last me till death at least, I'll offer a few suggestions from my own slow and blundering course. I make no claim for their wisdom or even their usefulness. Whether they'll prove merely private to me or available to a handful of others as ground for thought, I'd likely be the last to know; but at least I can try to keep them honest. Here then are the minimal facts that eventually worked for me, at least part of the time, and are working still. In all that follows, the pronoun *You* is aimed at me as much as any reader. I need steady coaching; I'm never home-free. And when I refer to physical paralysis, I often suspect that other kinds of mind and body paralysis bring similar troubles with similar remedies.

Fairly late in the catastrophic phase of my illness, I began to understand three facts I'd known in theory since early childhood but had barely plumbed the reality of. They're things familiar to most adults who've bothered to watch the visible world and have sorted their findings with normal intelligence, but abstract knowledge tends to vanish in a crisis. And from where I've been, the three facts stand at the head of any advice I'd risk conveying to a friend confronted with grave illness or other physical and psychic trauma.

1. You're in your present calamity alone, far as this life goes. If you want a way out, then dig it yourself, if there turns out to be any trace of a way. Nobody— least of all a doctor—can rescue you now, not from the deeps of your own mind, not once they've stitched your gaping wound.
2. Generous people—true practical saints, some of them boring as root canals—are waiting to give you everything on Earth but your main want, which is simply *the person you used to be*.
3. But you're not that person now. Who'll you be tomorrow? And who do you propose to be from here to the grave, which may be hours or decades down the road?

The first two facts take care of themselves; if you haven't already known them in spades and obeyed their demands, they'll blow you nearly down till you concede their force. Harder though, and even more urgent, admit the third fact as soon as you can. No child of the doomed Romanov czar, awaiting rescue or brutal death in 1917, was more firmly banished from a former life than you are now. Grieve for a decent limited time over whatever parts of your old self you know you'll miss.

That person is dead as any teen-aged Marine drilled through the forehead in an Asian jungle; any Navy Seal with his legs blown off, halved for the rest of the time he gets; any woman mangled in her tenderest parts, unwived, unmothered, unlovered and shorn. Have one hard cry, if the tears will come. Then stanch the grief, by whatever legal means. Next find your way to be somebody else, the next viable you—a stripped-down whole other clear-eyed person, realistic as a sawed-off shotgun and thankful for air, not to speak of the human kindness you'll meet if you get normal luck.

Your mate, your children, your friends at work—anyone who knew or loved you in your old life—will be hard at work in the fierce endeavor to revive your old self, the self they recall with love or respect. Their motives are frequently admirable, and at times that effort counts for a lot—they prove that you're valued and wanted at least—but again their care is often a brake on the way you must go. At the crucial juncture, when you turn toward the future, they'll likely have little help to offer; and it's no fault of theirs (they were trained like you, in inertia).

More likely they'll stall you in the effort to learn who you need to be now and how to be him or her by tomorrow or Monday at the latest. Yet if you don't discover that next appropriate incarnation of who you must be, and then *become* that person at a stiff trot, you'll be no good whatever again to the ruins of your old self nor to any friend or mate who's standing beside you in hopes of a hint that you're feeling better this instant and are glad of company.

*

The kindest thing anyone could have done for me, once I'd finished five weeks' radiation, would have been to look me square in the eye and say this clearly, "Reynolds Price is dead. Who will you be now? Who *can* you be and how can you get there, double-time?" Cruel and unusable as it might have sounded in the wake of trauma, I think its truth would have snagged deep in me and won my attention eventually, far sooner than I managed to find it myself. Yet to this day, with all the kindnesses done for me, no one has so much as hinted that news in my direction; and I've yet to meet another dazed person who's heard it when it was needed most—*Come back to life, whoever you'll be. Only you can do it.*

How you'll manage that huge transformation is your problem though and nobody else's. Are there known techniques for surviving a literal hairpin turn in the midst of a life span—or early or late—without forgetting the better parts of who you were? What are the thoughts and acts required to turn your dead self inside-out into something new and durably practical that, however strange, is the creature demanded by whatever hard facts confront you now? So far as I've heard, nobody else knows—or knows in a way they can transfer to others. If they know, I haven't encountered their method. I'll go on sketching my own course then.

I've made it clear that the first strong props beneath my own collapse were prayer, a single vision that offered me healing, the one word *More* when I asked "What now?" and a frail continuing sense of purpose, though my hungry self often worked to drown any voice that might otherwise have reached me from the mind of God or plain common sense. But I well understand how that kind of help is all but incommunicable to anyone else not so inclined from childhood. If belief in an ultimately benign creator who notices his creatures is available to you, you may want to try at first to focus your will on the absolute first ground-level question to ask him, her or faceless it. Again, that's not "Why me?" but "What next?"

In general the human race has believed that a God exists who is at least partly good. Recent polls have shown that a huge majority of Americans pray in some form daily; even many self-defined atheists pray apparently. And thousands of years of testimony from sane men and women is serious evidence, if not full proof, that God may consult you in unannounced moments. If he does so at all, it will likely mean that you've taken prior pains to know him. He'll almost surely lurk beyond you in heavy drapery with face concealed. He's likewise announced, in most major creeds, his availability for fox-hole conversions. Yet foxhole occupants are often faced with his baffling slowness to answer calls, or they reach a perpetual busy signal or a cold-dead line. Again, the answer to most prayers is *No.*

My own luck here was long prepared, from early child-hood; but as with all sorts of invisible luck, there have been forced treks these past ten years when I all but quit and begged to die. Even then though I'd try to recall a passage of daunting eloquence in the thirtieth chapter of the Book of Deuteronomy where the baffling God of Jews and Christians says

> I call Heaven and Earth to witness against you today
> that I have set life and death in front of you, bless-
> ing and curse. Therefore choose life so that you and
> your seed may last to love the Lord your God. . . .

Clear as the offered choice is, such a reach for life is another tall order, especially for a human in agonized straits. But even if you omit the last phrase from God's proposition (that you last to love him, even if you're a confirmed disbeliever), you're still confronted with another iron fact. The visible laws of physical nature are willing you to last as long as you can. Down at the core, you almost certainly want to survive.

You're of course quite free to balk that wish, by killing yourself and ending your physical will to endure; but amazingly few pained people choose death by suicide. And fewer still consider the strangeness of their endless moaning when death is so easy. To be sure, either God or the laws of nature will eventually force you to fall and die. But that event can tend to itself, with slim help from you. Meanwhile whether you see yourself as the temporary home of a deathless soul or as the short-term compound of skin and bone called *Homo sapiens*, your known orders are simply to *Live*. Never give death a serious hearing till its ripeness forces your final attention and dignified nod. It will of course take you screaming if it must, if you insist.

And keep control of the air around you. Many well-meaning mates, lovers and friends will stand by, observing that you're in the throes of blind denial—*Give up. Let go.* Get them out of your sight and your hearing with red-hot haste; use whatever force or fury it takes. Then try to choose life. Then see who you can live with now.

In my case, life has meant steady work, work sent by God but borne on my own back and on the wide shoulders of friends who want me to go on living and have helped me with a minimum of tears and no sign of pity. My work admittedly has been of the sort that, when it's available, permits deep absorption. It's also brought me sufficient money to guarantee time for further work and appropriate space in which to do it. Since childhood I've been subject to frequent sixteen-hour days, chained to an easel or desk in my home and glad to be grounded. Some other home workers have similar luck—gardening, wood-craft, pottery, sewing, cooking, the ceaseless daily needs of a family. Even the man or woman who works in an office or mill, even at the dullest repetitive task, has a ready-made routine for muting painful cries from the self.

The killing dead-ends are strewn all around you in the idle or physically weak aftermath of calamity itself, the stunned hours of blank wall-gazing that eagerly await you. Find any legal way to avoid my first mistake, which was sitting still in cooperation with the cancer's will to finish me fast. Play cutthroat card games, leave the house when you can, go sit in the park near children at play, read to children in a cancer ward, go donate whatever strength you've got to feeding the hungry or tending the millions worse off than you. I wish to God I had—any legal acts to break the inward gaze at my withering self.

As soon as I could walk after my first surgery, Allan Friedman urged me to make immediate plans to return to campus—put a cot in my office, go there daily, deal with the mail and at least see my colleagues for lunch and small talk, feel free to call on him anytime he kept clinic hours or to phone whenever. What he failed to know as a busy surgeon was, I'd never written ten words in my campus office and couldn't think of trying—I'd merely be alone in a different building. Since it was sum-mer, most of my colleagues had fled their offices, unlike physicians who work all seasons; and Duke Hospital, as a place to visit, felt like sure death.

But now I know Friedman was more than half right. Professors were not my only colleagues; in the long years of my life at Duke, I'd built a sizable village of friends—members of the post-office staff, workers in the dining rooms, bookstores, librarians, campus cops. Any trip to campus would have involved my meeting their usual hardheaded cheer; I'd have heard their own tales of good and bad luck. (Not at all incidentally, one of my friends on the postal staff phoned me one Sunday, a few weeks into the ordeal, and said that the members of his church had just agreed—they'd bring me all my meals, five days a week. I was amazed and thanked them firmly but declined the offer, at least for then.)

Surely I should have forced myself to move outward from the menacing house far sooner than I did. Though I couldn't drive, and was years away from thinking of an appropriate car, I might at least have ridden with my friend Betsy Cox to her regular stints at a homeless shelter in downtown Durham. I could have made bologna sandwiches as fast as she and listened to stories harder than mine; and if I wet my pants in the process, well, who the hell hasn't? Couldn't I have gone out and learned some useful degree of proportion, setting my woes in the midst of the world, yet still have kept my silent hours for learning how much damage I'd taken and how to build on it?

Anyone for whom such recommendations seem overly rosy should not miss the point. Your chance of rescue from any despair lies, if it lies anywhere, in your eventual decision to abandon the deathwatch by the corpse of your old self and to search out a new inhabitable body. The old *Theologica Germanica* knew that "nothing burns in Hell but the self"—above all, the old self broiling in the fat of its endless self-pity.

By very slow inches, as I've said, the decision to change my life forced itself on me; and I moved ahead as if a path was actually there and would stretch on a while. As truly as I could manage here in an intimate memoir, without exposing the private gifts of men and women who never asked to perform in my books, I've tried to map the lines of that change and the ways I traveled toward the reinvention and reassembly of a life that bears some relations with a now-dead life but is radically altered, trimmed for a whole new wind and route. A different life and—till now at least, as again I've said—a markedly better way to live, for me and for my response to most of the people whom my life touches.

I've tested that word *better* for the stench of sentimentality, narcissism, blind optimism or lunacy. What kind of twisted fool, what megalomaniac bucking for canonization, would give his strong legs and control of a body that gave him fifty-one years' good service with enormous amounts of sensory pleasure (a body that played a sizable part in winning him steady love from others) and would then surrender normal control of a vigorous life in an ample house and far beyond it in exchange for what?—two legs that serve no purpose but ballast to a numb torso and the rest of a body that acts as a magnet to no one living, all soaked in corrosive constant pain?

I know that this new life is better for me, and for most of my friends and students as well, in two measurable ways. First, paraplegia with its maddening limitations has forced a degree of patience and consequent watchfulness on me, though as a writer I'd always been watchful. Shortly after my own paralysis, I heard two of Franklin Roosevelt's sons say that the primary change in their father, after polio struck him in mid-life and grounded him firmly, was an increased patience and a willingness to listen. If you doubt that patience must follow paralysis, try imagining that you can't escape whoever manages to cross your doorsill.

Forced to sit, denied the easy flight that legs provide, you either learn patience or you cut your throat, or you take up a bludgeon and silence whoever's in reach at the moment. As I survived the black frustration of so many new forms of powerlessness, I partly learned to sit and attend, to watch and taste whatever or whomever seemed likely or needy, far more closely than I had in five decades. The pool of human evidence that lies beneath my writing and teaching, if nothing more, has grown in the wake of that big change.

Then the slow migration of a sleepless and welcome sexuality from the center of my life to the cooler edge has contributed hugely to the increased speed and volume of my work, not to speak of the gradual resolution of hungers that—however precious to mind and body— had seemed past feeding. It's the sex that's moved, in fact, not the eros. The sense of some others as radiant and magnetic bodies, bodies that promise pleasure and good, is if anything larger in my life than before.

And especially now that my remaining senses are free from the heavy damper of methadone, all other pain drugs and the muscle relaxant baclofen that stunned me for seven years, specific desire does come again and find expression in new ways that match the rewards of the old. But the fact that, in ten years since the tumor was found, I've completed thirteen books—I'd published a first twelve in the previous twenty-two years—would seem at least another demonstration that human energy, without grave loss, may flow from one form into another and win the same consoling gains. (The question of why and how I was able to increase my rate is unanswerable, by me anyhow—a race with death and silence, a massive rerouting of sexual energy would be the easy answers. But if I was racing, I never felt chased; panic came elsewhere but never in my work. On the contrary, I sense strongly that the illness itself either unleashed a creature within me that had been restrained and let him run at his own hungry will; or it planted a whole new creature in place of the old.)

There've been other, maybe more private, gains. Once the hand wringers and ambulance chasers disperse from your side, you begin to feel and eventually savor the keener attentions of old friends who feel a complicated new duty to stand in closer. It's a duty that you have the duty to lighten, as Simone Weil said in her haunting law of friendship—

Our friends owe us what we think they will give us. We must forgive them this debt.

In a country as addicted to calamitous news as America now, word of your illness or imminent death will likely draw not just a ring of crows—not all of whom are eager to feed—but likewise a flock of serious watchers. Both halves of my written work, the books from 1962 to '84 and those thereafter, have benefited from new readers summoned by word of an ordeal survived, however briefly. When I traveled across the states in the spring of '92, following the publication of *Blue Calhoun*—twenty-three readings in fourteen cities—I caught for the first time in the eyes of strangers a certain intense eagerness of response that I doubt was won by my gray hair alone. A certified gimp, in working order, is often accorded an unearned awe which he may be forgiven for enjoying a moment till he rolls on past the nearest mirror and adjusts his vision for colder reality.

I'm left today, as I write this page, with an odd conclusion that's risky to state. But since it's not only thoroughly true but may well prove of use to another, I'll state it baldly—*I've led a mainly happy life.* I can safely push further. *I've yet to watch another life that seems to have brought more pleasure to its owner than mine has to me.* And that claim covers all my years except for the actual eye of the storm I've charted, from the spring of 1984 till fall '88.

I'm the son of brave magnanimous parents who'd have offered both legs in hostage for mine, if they'd been living when mine were required. I'm the brother of a laughing openhanded man with whom I've never exchanged an angry adult word nor wanted to. I'm the cousin of a woman who, with her husband, offered to see me through to the grave. I'm the neighbor of a couple who offered to share my life, however long I lasted. I'm the ward of a line of responsible assistants who've moved into my home and life at twelve-month intervals, taken charge of both the house and me and insured a safe and favorable atmosphere for ongoing work. I'm the friend of many more spacious and lively souls than I've earned. I've had, and still have, more love—in body and mind—than I dreamed of in my lone boyhood.

Doctors of superb craft and technical judgment, whatever their faults of attention and sympathy, ousted a lethal thing from my spine. Other resourceful attendants nursed me through pitch-black nights of roaring pain. An annual lot of intelligent students throws down a welcome gauntlet to me—*Give us all you've got, no discount for pain.* The unseen hand of the source of all has never felt absent as long as a week, and I share the sense of the holiday-painter as she finishes her canvas at the end of Virginia Woolf's *To the Lighthouse*—"I have had my vision." Mine was a vision of healing that's remained in force for a decade full, at the least, of work.

So though I travel for work and pleasure, here I sit

most weeks at work toward the end of ten years rocked with threats and hair-breadth rescues. Though I make no forecast beyond today, annual scans have gone on showing my spine clear of cancer—clear of visible growing cells at least (few cancer veterans will boast of a "cure"). When Allan Friedman's physician-wife heard the story of my continuing recovery at my sixtieth-birthday party, she said to Allan "But that's miraculous." Allan faced her, grinned and said "You could say that."

I've long since weaned myself from all drugs but a small dose of antidepressant, an aspirin to thin my blood, an occasional scotch or a good red wine and a simple acid to brace my bladder against infection. I write six days a week, long days that often run till bedtime; and the books are different from what came before in more ways than age. I sleep long nights with few hard dreams, and now I've outlived both my parents. Even my handwriting looks very little like the script of the man I was in June of '84. Cranky as it is, it's taller, more legible, with more air and stride. It comes down the arm of a grateful man.

Relevant Poems

THE DREAM OF A HOUSE

There seems no question the house is mine.
I'm told it first at the start of the tour—
"This is yours, understand. Meant for you.
Permanent." I nod gratitude,
Containing the flower of joy in my mouth—
I knew it would come if I waited, in time.
It's now all round me—and I catalog blessings
Tangible as babies: the floors wide teak
Boards perfectly joined, the walls dove plaster.
At either end a single picture,
Neither a copy—Piero's *Nativity*
With angel glee-club, Vermeer's pregnant girl
In blue with her letter. Ranks of books
On the sides—old Miltons, Tolstoys, *Wuthering*
Heights, Ackermann's *Oxford*. A holograph
Copy of Keats's "To Autumn." All roles
Of Flagstad, Leontyne Price in order
On tape, with photographs. Marian Anderson
At Lincoln Memorial, Easter 1939.
A sense of much more, patiently humming.
My guide gives me that long moment,
Then says "You've got your life to learn
This. I'll show you the rest."

I follow and the rest is normal house.
Necessary living quarters—clean
With a ship's scraped-bone economy. Bedroom
Cool as a cave, green bath,

Steel kitchen. We end in a long
Bright hall, quarry-tiled—
Long window at the far end
On thick woods in sunlight.
The guide gives a wave of consignment—
"Yours"—though he still hasn't smiled.
I ask the only question I know—
"Alone?" He waits, puzzled maybe
(For the first time I study him—a lean man,
Ten years my junior, neat tan clothes:
A uniform?). So I say again
"Alone?—will I be here alone?"
Then he smiles with a breadth that justifies his wait.
"Not from here on," he says. "That's ended too."
But he doesn't move to guide me farther.
I stand, thinking someone will burst in on us
Like a blond from a cake; and I reel off
Twenty-six years of candidates,
Backsliders till now. Silence stretches
Till he points to a closed door three steps
Beyond us.

I cannot go. After so much time—
Begging and vigils. He takes my elbow
And pulls me with him to an ordinary door,
Black iron knob. I only stand.
He opens for me—an ordinary hall
Closet: shelf lined with new hats,
Coats racked in corners. In the midst
Of tweeds and seersuckers, a man is
Nailed to a T-shaped rig—
Full-grown, his face eyelevel with mine,
Eyes clamped. He has borne on a body
No stronger than mine every
Offense a sane man would dread—
Flailed, pierced, gouged, crushed—

But he has the still bearable sweet
Salt smell of blood from my own finger,
Not yet brown, though his long
Hair is stiff with clots, flesh blue.

The guide has never released my arm.
Now he takes it to the face. I don't resist.
The right eyelid is cool and moist.
I draw back slowly and turn to the guide.

Smile more dazzling than the day outside,
He says "Yours. Always."

I nod my thanks, accept the key.
From my lips, enormous, a blossom spreads
At last—white, smell strong as
New iron chain: gorgeous,
Lasting, fills the house.

THE DREAM OF REFUSAL

I've come on foot through dark dense as fur
(Clean, dry but pressed to my mouth)
To find my mother's father's house
In Macon, N.C. I know he's been dead
Since she was a girl, but—stronger—I know
A secret's here I must face to live.

At the end of seventy miles I see it,
Though the dark's unbroken and no light shows
From any tall window or the open door.
I pull myself through the rooms by hand—
All dead, empty, no stick or thread,
Not the house I loved in childhood.

And no more hint of a vital secret
Than noon sun stamps on a working hand.
I forget my life is staked on this hunt,
That these walls store dried acts or words
To kill or save precisely me who pass
Fool-fearless and out again—the yard, lighter dark.

I'm leaving the place and have reached the thicket
Of shrubs near the road. I step through the last
Clear space that can still be called my goal—
My mother's father's home in Macon.
I lift my foot to enter freedom
(And death? I no longer think of death).

*

Behind me I feel a quick condensation—
Sizable presence barely humming
In furious motion. Fear thrusts up in me
Like rammed pack-ice. But I know again
Why I'm here at all, and slowly I turn
Onto whatever deadly shadow waits.

What seems a small man—blackhaired, young—
Crouches in yellow glow he makes,
A smoke from his skin. I know at once
His motion is dance; that he dances every
Instant he breathes, huddled ecstatic.
His hands are empty. He beckons me.

I know he will make his thrust any moment;
I cannot guess what aim it will take.
Then as—appalled—I watch him quiver,
He says "Now you must learn the bat dance."
I know he has struck. It is why I came.
In one long silent step, I refuse and turn toward home.

I will walk all night. I will not die of cancer.
Nothing will make me dance in that dark.

THE EEL

1. 25 July 1984

Mother, the name of this thing is the eel.
It is one foot long, thick as a pencil
And lives in the upper half of my spine—
Ambitious now to grow all ways.
Every atom of me it turns to it
Is me consumed.
                     Yet it's been there always,
Original part—which is my first news
For you in years. It came in the first
Two cells of me, a gift therefore
From you or Father—my secret twin
Through those hard years that threatened desolation
But found rescue in dumb resort
To inner company, a final friend
Concealed at the core on which I'd press
Companionship, brief cries for help.

It helped. My purple baby convulsions
That got more notice than a four-car wreck,
Weak arms that balked a playground career
And kept me in for books and art,
Toilet mishaps, occasional blanks—
Tidy gifts to aim and guide me.
I steadily thanked it and on we came,
Paired for service fifty years.

*

Now it means to be me. And has made huge gains.
I'm numb as brass over one and a half legs,
All my upper back, groin, now my scalp;
Both arms are cringing weaker today,
And I walk like a stove-up hobo at dawn.
What broke the bond, the life-in-life
That saw us both through so much good?

Mother of us both, you left here
Nineteen years ago—your own brain
Drowning itself, eager blood—
And prayers to the dead are not my line;
But a question then: have you learned a way,
There where you watch, to help me kill
This first wombmate; strangle, fire out
Every trace of one more heirloom
Grinding jaws? Do you choose me to live?

Struggle to tell.

2. 26 July 1984

Mother, this man is now all eel.
Each morning he's hauled upright to a chair
And sits all day by a window near trees.
Pale leafshine honors the green of his skin,
The black-bead eyes. He wants no more;
His final triumph stokes him with permanent
Fuel for the years of wait, twitched
Only by drafts, damp rubs by his nurse
Or mild waves of gravity flushing the compact
Waste from his bore.
                         He does not know you
Nor the twin he ate. He could not name
The taste of joy, but he licks it slowly
In his bone hook-jaws. He thinks only "Me.
I became all me."

3. 26–30 July 1984

Mother, this man will stay a man.
He knows it three ways. First, he's watched
A credible vision—no dream rigged for comfort
But a visible act in a palpable place
Where Jesus washed and healed his wound,
The old eel sluiced out harmless in the lake.
    Then a woman he trusts like a high stone wall
Phoned to say "You will not die.
You'll live and work to a ripe old age"—
And quoted Psalm 91's reckless vow,
He will give his angels charge over you
To guard you in all your ways.
    Then he knows what a weight of good rests in him,
The stocked warehouses of fifty-one years—
Waiting for export, barter, gift;
Lucid poems of fate and grace,
Novels like patient hands through the maze,
Honest memories of his own ruins and pleasures
(All human, though many blind and cruel).

Years more to teach the famished children
Rising each spring like throats of flowers,
Asking for proof that life is literally
Viable in time.
              Long years more
To use what I think I finally glimpse—
The steady means of daily love
In daily life: the patience, trust,
Suspended fear, to choose one soul
And stand nearby and say "Be you.
Be near but *you.*"
            And thereby praise,

The Eel

Thank, recompense the mind of God
That sent me, Mother, through straits of your
Own hectic womb and into life
To fight this hardest battle now—
A man upright and free to give,
In desperate need.

HAWK HILL, FOR WILLIAM SINGER

August dusk. We rest on the green porch,
Yellowjackets and ants at our knees—
You in from work, ready to cook
The dinner I can't: I three-fourths through
The eightieth sick-day, weaker still;
We cheering a milestone with smooth Glenlivet:
Eleven years of peace and war,
Our squalls and calms. The hidden thrush
In the big beech behind us pauses to plan
His billionth variation on the five notes
Stamped in his throat.
                                    You face me and say
"*Real time*," then add with customary
Unbarked candor "Whether you make it
Or not, these days were real time"—
Twelve days in which you've fed me squarely,
Dried my bedsore, each night stripped
My slack-legs for baby-sleep (that sound and brief):
No word or sign of balk or grievance,
The flawless service dreamed by kings.

Whether I make it or not, old struggler
(Treasured as any, with all our scars),
Feel it hereafter as all real time—
All one linked try to tread one void.
We pay for it now.

AN AFTERLIFE, 1953–1988

Thirty-five years, a gory rake—
My parents scrubbed in laughing prime,
The Kennedys, King, sixty thousand
Baffled sons in Vietnam,
The countless thousand sons they offed,
Mobs of flower-handed girls
Keening for rescue, blazing kids,
A normal stock of routine pillage,
Lunacy, rapture, genocide, famine;
And then my legs unstrung, both frozen,
Me flung down to sit through what
May be of time, need, gift.
　　　But here, a clear warm day, I come
On a hare-brained backward lunge, trucked up
In a black wheelchair by chuckling friends
To scout my youth and hunt the cabin
Where I passed a slow ten summer weeks
With boys smooth as baby birds—
Mild, still naked-hearted toward
A world they'd barely dreamed was mad.

We've got a key from the owner's son;
And once we pass a final gate
Where hemlocks start, I know each rock,
Each fern primeval.
　　　　　　　　No tears yet
But a dry amazement humps up hot
In my dry mouth. When we break in
On the heart of the place, it's beating still
Though derelict for more than a decade.

206

The eyeless rake only groomed this hill
Where I worked my twenty-first summer—guide
And shield of a dozen tads, ten to twelve,
In a likable bonded warehouse and playground
For bored sprouts in the dogday swelter:
Summer camp.
                              Sequoyah after
The red inventor of Cherokee writing,
Laid up half a mountainside
In the floating Smokies by a fierce-eyed saint
And ramrod dreamer—Walton "Chief" Johnson
Never saw a boy whose timbers he
Couldn't shiver and brace for stiff headwinds:
Manhood! Seize it! God's high hope!
Your very name is on His *lips!*

Chief's daunted too, buried uphill
In magnanimous block-high hemlocks
Straight as the hope he nursed for man.
The swarms of boys are random-sown
Through a turgid world that may or may not
Be one amp of voltage brighter
For his husky ardor, sleepless labor,
The force of this nursery he gouged by will
From granite and the hearts of trees.
        I've been away since that last morning,
August 1953, when I
Left to lurk for two more years
At home and college; then the headlong
Spiky trail of my getaway, the mottled
Roll of Chased and Caught—trawling
Love in phosphorescent cities,
Unthinkable limbs and music dense
As baled swansdown or sunbaked mire—
Through that much time: no bitter month.

*

Same eye today, same skull—I hunt
Chief's house, the office, sick bay, lodge,
Library, crafts house, breezy low dining hall,
Oval ballfield, a waving swell
Of foot-deep turf uphill to the cabins
Propped on stilts.
                    I try to see
Two hundred yards toward where I guess
My cabin stood. Young blue cedars
Fog the view, but I point that way.
    And my tall friend says "Here you go."
Two more join and, while I cheerfully
Yell "No need," they lug me up.
The chair rolls game on ground rough as gator
Hide.

            It's there. Steps rotted, roof pocked,
Charming as a hatchet-built filigree box
But efficient as watchworks, host to nothing
Bigger than mice, squirrels, the brindle
Panther.
            A friend says "Ready?"
                                I think
He means "To roll downhill." And set
On stemming a risky flood, I say "You
Bet."
            Three bearers lift me, levitate
Three pulpy steps, park me safe
Inside.
            Thick air, cool as evening,
Brown as dusk—there, *here*
I finally am—thirty-five ticking
Years down a ring road.
                        The eight
Bunks swim up first from murk—
Four two-tiered six-foot canvas slings

That once stretched taut to sleep light bodies.
All but one are ready to serve
This moment—vacant, clean and dry
(One's torn and fallen, the one that bore
My sole bedwetter, a chunky towhead).
    Mine, the right-top sling by the door,
Suddenly stops my hungry eyes—
The boy I was those seventy nights,
Crusty with love as a cross with blood.
Hurried taps of the pressure valve
Would spare my mind, my mustang body,
Its devastation one more day;
Then through six hundred dreaming hours—
Tads sighing round me—I'd build designs
For my doomed try at knotting myself
In Gordian toils with a lanky blond,
Noble as Neptune, healthy as lye
And bent on yielding me nothing but shame
When what I craved was joint safety.

(*Safety!* The eros-octane in me,
Spilled and lit, would have jacked the crest
Of this hefty outcrop a quarter-mile higher
In chattering dark and crazed the skins
Of all live creatures in a five-mile arc
Like air-thin china in a runaway kiln.)

One friend, a camper years after me,
Says "Where's the plaque with your boys' names?"
    I say "Plaques came well after my time"
And look to a tidy line of boards
Nailed to the eaves. Dim as we are
With me hunched low, I see no words
And turn again to study my bunk—
The night I rolled in after twelve,
Back from a long day-off in Asheville,

And vaulted into my covers to feel
The chill depths lined with chillier rocks.
Both feet clenched, suspecting worse—
A snapping turtle or frosty snake
Mad for heat and a chance at fury,
Fond welcome home from the comatose boys.

A friend says "*Ah!* The Great Memory falters!"
He's stretching a match to the webby heights—
A brown plaque, maybe nine by five
And older than most, apparently blank.
But then he reads, a blind child groping:
"1953—Reynolds Price, Counselor—
Paul Auston, Jim Avary,
Ed Grimsley, Buddy McKenzie,
Tommy Moore, Raiford Baxley,
Terry Brookshire, George Harrell,
Jonathan Lindsay, Lester Shepherd.
Ten-week campers: Bill Barrington
And Randy Floyd."

Stunned as a beef at the abattoir door,
I hear the dead names hurtle through me—
Searing, healing, possibly both.
      As six friends gang at the wonder site,
I sink in merciful isolation
And watch a line of figures scramble
From an unsuspected open grave—

A dozen boys, twelve heads for the names,
Big teeth, chopped hair, a team of voices:
None cracked, each laughing, not a tear
In the loaded days.
                              And none from me,
All-Purpose Font, those days or now.

Halfway uphill, jigged in pain,
I'd wondered coldly why I shanghaied
A weekend's rest for a retrograde,
Dead-sure to appall—*Broke-Down Me
Hunts Me at the Full*: hard boy, primed
For a life that looked in this pure air
Plainly unending, a noonday glide,
But ran a quick hot thirty-one years
Toward an unmapped iron murderous wall
That ended me.
                          Here though, reborn—
Amply friended, spoiled as a pasha,
Unmanned in a fecund afterlife—
I watch the boys' eyes sink again;
And I hear these lean words, mute though clear,
The pitch of Hopkins' "Felix Randal":
*How far from then forethought of, all
Thy more boisterous years.*
                          Boisterous, good
To see, starved as a stoat and wild
To couple—for *chance*, bliss, mayhem—
Impeccably kind and cruel as the child
I'd only just been: now this snowcapped
Hulk on wheels.

              *How far from then
Forethought of*. But grand.

Before a friend can turn from the wall
And smile down toward me, I watch the coals
Of my sequestered phoenix pyre
Flare inside me, light for every
Soul in darkness.
                          Grander still—
Young, I stood here, cocked but blank.

An Afterlife, 1953–1988

Old, I sit in a hole my green
Self cut in this clean air, seeing now
In my new head a sight my green mind
Never dreamed—the eyes, lips, talons,
Rampant sons and muffled names
Of incontestable angels hid
Past this roof, past the blue abyss—
From all but me, the sole relay
For man on Earth and earthly beasts
Of seraph hymns in adoration,
Praise, undying blame and glee.
I breast their scalding tides of anguish,
Drink their essence—pain and promise,
Grace and torment—
                        Know the back
Of God's right hand (my teeth still taste
His acrid blood), know Death will somedays
Stall at a door if strong eyes bay him;
Know he marks strict time in silence,
Final friend.

                        One live friend moves,
"Sure, let's take it." His broad hand reaches
For the coded plaque still aimed at time,
A plucky voyager.
                        My own hand lifts,
Unspeakably strong, to stop him there.
"It lives here. Leave it." I trust they see
The choice is mine, a power earned
In walking toward the boiling core
On shards of broken mirrors barefoot;
Then returning, charred but me.
Let this pine board endure its earned
Fate in place here—bearing its news
To silence, nestlings, the stone-deaf adder.

                        *

212

My friend's hand drops, though no friend kneels
And no head nods to the solar flare
That fuses light herself with time
Behind my brow, this bony ridge
That bears the fire—outright knowledge
Of how to stay and how to leave,
What to hold and when to loose:
The only secret, *utter loss*;
Glad surrender of every hope but the life
That, breath by slow sweet breath, confounds
An end.

       I blink a long instant,
Rig my grinning mask to join them—
Affable gimp.

        Two more minutes,
They bear me out and down again,
Heavy but likewise potent as pig iron.
Flung toward dark, a homing bird.

REYNOLDS PRICE

Reynolds Price was born in Macon, North Carolina in 1933. Reared and educated in the public schools of his native state, he earned an A.B. *summa cum laude* from Duke University, graduating first in his class. In 1955 he traveled as a Rhodes Scholar to Merton College, Oxford University to study English literature. After three years and the B.Litt. degree, he returned to Duke where he continues to teach as James B. Duke Professor of English.

In 1962 his novel *A Long and Happy Life* appeared. It received the William Faulkner Award for a notable first novel and has never been out of print. Since, he has published more than two dozen books. In 1986 his novel *Kate Vaiden* received the National Book Critics Circle Award; his most recent novel, *Blue Calhoun*, appeared in 1992. His *Collected Stories* followed in 1993. He has also published volumes of poems, plays, essays, translations from the Bible, and the memoir *Clear Pictures*; and he has written for the screen, for television, and the texts for songs by James Taylor.

His television play *Private Contentment* was commissioned by "American Playhouse" and appeared in its premiere season on PBS. His trilogy of plays, *New Music*, premiered at the Cleveland Play House in 1989; and its three plays have been produced throughout the country, as has a newer play, *Full Moon*, his sixth. In the summer of 1993 he served as host for PBS's two-hour documentary on the ninth Van Cliburn International Piano Competition in Fort Worth, Texas; and Charles Guggenheim, three-time Oscar winner for the documentary, has recently completed a film about him.

He is a member of the American Academy of Arts and Letters, and his books have appeared in sixteen languages.